For Women Only

For Women Only

Carla Ferrigno's Total Shape-Up Program

Carla Ferrigno

Contemporary Books, Inc.
Chicago

Library of Congress Cataloging in Publication Data

Ferrigno, Carla.
   For women only.

   Bibliography: p.
   Includes index.
   1. Exercise for women.   2. Physical fitness for
women.   3. Women—Nutrition.   I. Title.
RA781.F47   1982   613'.04244   82-45442
ISBN 0-8092-5660-6

All photos by John Balik and printed by Isgo Lepejian,
Burbank, California.

Contents

To my husband Lou, whose strength has taught me to ascend my dreams, and **to my daughter Shanna,** who gave me a new chapter in my book and in my life.

Foreword

As both a beneficiary of the health and fitness lifestyle and a long-term devotee of this way of life, I can tell you that you will receive an incredible array of positive benefits from maintaining regular exercise habits and following a well-balanced, health-promoting diet. By following a health and fitness lifestyle, you can actually fulfill your mental, physical, and emotional potential.

A large number of men and women idle along at less than 50 percent of their true potential. They are chronically fatigued, suffer from constant minor health problems and occasionally from major illnesses, are often depressed and out of sorts, are overweight or underweight, lack the muscle strength necessary to perform ordinary daily tasks, lack confidence, and smoke and drink excessively.

If I told you that you could easily have an unlimited amount of energy, enough strength to carry two heavy bags of groceries from your car to your kitchen, clear skin, an even temperament, abundant self-confidence, the ebullience to dance half the night, and then the ability to sleep deeply and without interruption all night, you would think me to be ready for the funny farm. But these benefits, as well as scores more, can soon be yours if you choose to embrace the health and fitness way of life.

When I first became aware of systematic exercise and health-promoting dietary practices at the age of fourteen, I was painfully thin and weak. I was so introverted and shy that I couldn't even talk to a girl. But within two years of following a health and fitness lifestyle—with particular emphasis placed on weight training—I had normalized my appearance and grown much stronger physically. Such a dramatic improvement greatly augmented my self-confidence, which in turn drew me out of my shell.

Eventually, I became an extroverted, athletic, and widely respected person, which would have been totally unthinkable at the time I began exercising and monitoring my diet. With time I won the Mr. America title and two Mr. Universe titles, played pro football, and even won my preliminary heat of ABC Television's "Superstars" competition. Later I placed quite high against the world's greatest athletes in the "Superstars" finals. Before adopting a health and fitness way of life, I would have been afraid even to talk to one of these famous athletes.

My body became so well-developed that I was signed for a four-season run as CBS Television's Incredible Hulk. As a result, I'm well known both nationally and internationally, I've married an intelligent and beautiful woman, and fathered a healthy, active daughter. I owe all of my successes in life directly to my adherence to a health and fitness lifestyle. If I hadn't adopted this way of life, I would probably still be an introvert, only dreaming of doing some of the things I have done so far.

I am fortunate that my wife, Carla, had adopted the health and fitness lifestyle many years before I met her. Carla was originally quite overweight, and she suffered from prolonged bouts of depression. But by adopting regular exercise habits and watching her diet, she slimmed down rapidly and became a veritable energy dynamo.

Even when Carla was pregnant with our daughter, she exercised regularly and worked at least an eight-hour day every day. And ultimately she presented me with a superbly healthy daughter.

I am sure that you will be inspired by Carla's success story and her clearly outlined instructions for pursuing your own health and fitness lifestyle. I sincerely hope that you will be inspired enough to make health and fitness part of your own life. If you do, you will soon harvest the benefits of such a lifestyle. If you profit from following

a health and fitness way of life even remotely as much as Carla, Shanna Victoria, and I have, you will be rich beyond all measure.

You have at your fingertips a guidebook to adopting your own health and fitness lifestyle. Go for it, and soon you will wake up to a new you!

Lou Ferrigno
May, 1982

For Women Only

1

A Philosophy
of Life

Would you like to stay young looking longer? Have clearer eyes and skin? Have fewer wrinkles and greater skin firmness? Have more strength and energy? Be physically fit? Feel less anxiety and stress? Look better in clothing? Rid your body of cellulite? Feel better about yourself?

If you answered "yes" to any or all of the above questions, you should definitely consider adopting the health and fitness way of life. By exercising regularly and correctly, maintaining good nutritional habits, and adopting a positive mental attitude, you will be living the health and fitness way. And as a result you will soon be able to claim for yourself the wonderful benefits just listed.

I was once in extremely poor health and physical condition. I was grossly overweight and terribly unhappy. I was far too heavy for my bone structure, and I lacked even the small amount of energy needed merely to make it through the day comfortably. In a word, I was a *mess.*

Fortunately, I took charge of my existence and began to exercise regularly. That in turn led me to adopt healthier eating habits and a better mental attitude toward my life. Soon I was looking and feeling much better than ever before. Life had become pleasure instead of drudgery.

Through regular exercise, a healthy diet, and an improved mental image of myself, my life totally changed for the better. I developed abundant self-confidence and began to enjoy thoroughly my newfound lifestyle. I began to believe in myself and was able to accomplish many things in my life that would have previously been impossible.

Later I met my husband, Lou Ferrigno, who is a former Mr. America and Mr. Universe title winner. He is totally committed to health and fitness, and a day doesn't go by when he's not doing at least a weight training session or an aerobic workout. Quite often he does both in the same day in his continuing effort to maintain superb physical condition and good health.

With Lou's encouragement and inspirational example, I began to intensify my physical activities. I added strength training with weights to my aerobic workouts, which had consisted of running, swimming, bicycling, roller skating, dancing, and aerobic exercise to music.

Lou and I even began to do a lot of our workouts together, which created a closeness between us that hadn't been there when we first met. Some of my most enjoyable moments have come while jogging around the UCLA running track with Lou, sprinting up and down a long set of sidewalk stairs near the beach in Santa Monica with him, or pumping iron with Lou in one of the many southern California gyms we frequent.

Within two or three weeks of beginning my intensified workouts, I was surprised to note that my body was firmer everywhere and I was looking and feeling far better than ever! My days became more and more enjoyable, and my energy flowed strongly and steadily for all of my waking hours. At the end of the day I was able to sleep more and more soundly, and I soon found that I needed less sleep to feel fully refreshed. Also, I quickly noticed how much Lou appreciated the new muscle tone and improved contours my body had taken on.

When I was pregnant with our daughter Shanna every woman friend who had already had a baby marveled at the ease with which I carried on all of my accustomed daily activities, even continuing to manage Lou's acting career and our myriad business affairs. Delivering Shanna was almost unbelievably easy due to my health and physical fitness. And less than six weeks after her birth I looked better physically than I had before becoming pregnant.

Because I follow a health and fitness lifestyle—as well as help my family follow it—I have entered a zone of "superfitness" that few women enjoy. And it's unfortunate that all women don't choose to experience such a natural high, because my workouts take no more than one hour a day, six days a week, and that time expenditure is easily compensated for by the shorter periods of sleep that I now need.

It takes no longer to prepare nutritionally healthy meals than it takes to fry some

greasy concoction that is guaranteed to clog your arteries with cholesterol plaque someday. And it's great to have a man around the house who enjoys and is easily pleased by simple, healthy foods.

The health and fitness way of life requires a lifetime commitment, which might conceivably put off some women. But I have found that the exercise sessions quickly become the most enjoyable part of a woman's day, and such a commitment becomes something to be desired rather than feared. I can assure you that after only one short month of following the health and fitness way of life you will be positively addicted to it for life.

Three Components of Health and Fitness

As mentioned earlier, there are three components of the health and fitness way of life: good nutrition; regular exercise; and a positive mental approach to life along with a systematic plan of stress reduction. Let's discuss each of these factors individually.

Good Nutrition

There is a saying that "you are what you eat." This is literally true, because every organ, bone, muscle, fluid, and tissue in your body is formed from the nutrients that you ingest. With this in mind, it makes good sense to feed your body only the best of nutrients. And this in turn builds the best possible body for you, in terms of both health and physical fitness.

In Chapter 2 we will discuss the wide range of nutritional factors you should consider and eventually incorporate into your diet. Briefly, however, I recommend eating fresh, low-fat, low-calorie, high-fiber foods, which will make you much healthier and enhance longevity.

Regular Exercise

Human bodies are very much like machines. If they are used regularly, they tend to work efficiently for life. But if they are neglected and left without exercise, they can begin to rust from disuse, the same as can an automobile parked for years in a farmer's field.

Chapter 4 will cover three major types of exercise—strength training (with weights), aerobic training (running, swimming, bicycling, etc.), and stretching workouts (yoga, flexibility exercises, etc.). When a woman is highly fit in each of these three areas she can be considered "superfit." Toward that end, Chapter 4 ends with a superfitness training program combining weight workouts, aerobic training, and flexibility exercise.

Positive Mental Approach and Stress Reduction

The mind is truly the master organ of your body, because it controls all of the body's voluntary and involuntary processes. In Chapter 3 you will learn how to program your mind positively to help you achieve your health and fitness goals. When your mind is properly programmed to maintain a positive mental attitude toward life, you'll find yourself becoming more and more happy with yourself.

As modern life has become increasingly complex, each of us has been forced to endure greater stress. And the harmful effects of stress on our minds and bodies have been well documented. Therefore, part of Chapter 3 is devoted to a discussion of how you can efficiently reduce the degree of stress that you feel each day.

Health = Wealth

There is a proverb that states, "If you don't have your health, you don't have anything." And with the health and fitness regimens outlined in this book, you will be able to maximize your chances of staying healthy and physically active well into your seventies and eighties. I'm sure that you know scores of men and women who would literally give *anything* for such health and vibrant longevity.

If you can, read through this book in one or two sittings. This should give you a good overall appreciation of what you'll need to do with nutrition, mental approach, and exercise to revamp your life for the better. Later you can go back and read each individual chapter more carefully, also referring to the bibliography at the back of this book for more detailed readings in each specific area. The most important chapters for now are the three that cover nutrition, mental approach, and exercise (Chapters 2–4).

If you have a relationship, and particularly if you have children, I strongly recommend reading Chapter 5, which covers couple and family fitness techniques. Nothing can equal the unique pleasures that you will receive from workouts taken with your loved ones. Even the elderly can be included in your family exercise sessions.

Low energy levels are quite a common complaint among women, and if this is a problem for you, read Chapter 6. That chapter tells you how to improve your energy flow. And in Chapter 7 we will deal with such uniquely female topics as exercise during menstruation and pregnancy and how exercise can improve your natural beauty without overusing cosmetics.

In the final chapter of this book is the transcript of an interview of me done by Bill Reynolds, editor-in-chief of *Muscle & Fit-*ness magazine and a widely read health and physical fitness authority. This particular interview flowed so well that it serves effectively to tie together all of the foregoing chapters as well as to answer the most common questions women ask me.

Now is an opportune time to wish you the best of luck with your health and fitness improvement efforts. You can definitely succeed by following the directions in this book, but the degree of your success will depend totally on you. Only you can faithfully follow these guidelines, but when you do you'll reap great and lasting rewards. Good luck and good health!

2

Nutrition for Better Health and Appearance

Among health-conscious women, nutrition is widely studied, avidly discussed, and largely misunderstood. And the quality of a woman's diet is responsible for at least 60 percent of her success in achieving buoyantly good health, optimum physical fitness, improved appearance, and inner happiness. It is logical, then, that simple, easily understood nutritional guidelines should be established in any book on the health and fitness lifestyle for women.

Throughout history literally hundreds of diets—most of them short-lived fads—have been used by women worldwide. In this chapter we will discuss those diets most frequently used by women today, pointing out which are most effective, which are healthy to follow, and which might cause harm to your body. Some weight-reduction diets are so unbalanced nutritionally that they can be very harmful to a woman's body!

Weight-reduction dieting is only the tip of the iceberg as far as nutrition is concerned. This chapter also contains discussions of weight-gain dieting, organic eating, how to judge food quality, low-sodium eating, and food supplementation. Also included is a comprehensive examination of the revolutionary cytotoxic diet, which when followed results in dramatic weight loss and almost miraculously improved health.

What Is Nutrition?

For the sake of definition, I consider *nutrition* to be an all-inclusive term referring to every philosophy and practice of taking food into the human body. A subdivision of nutrition is *diet,* a specific nutritional philosophy, of which there are many within the general category of nutrition.

Often the term *diet* is used exclusively to denote a weight-loss regimen of eating, but there are also weight-gaining diets and diets for maintaining body weight in a healthy manner. Similarly, the words *diet* and *nutrition* are frequently used interchangeably. In this book, however, we will always use the words *nutrition* and *diet* as defined above.

Since this chapter is almost exclusively about health-promoting nutrition, we need to define a healthy diet. A healthy diet is one having the following five elements:

5

1. It is made up of a wide variety of foods.
2. It consists primarily of fresh (nonfrozen, noncanned, nonpackaged, nonprocessed) foods.
3. The foods are eaten raw whenever possible or cooked minimally, since cooking destroys valuable enzymes in foods and turns organic nutrients into inorganic substances that are unusable in the human body.
4. Whenever possible, the foods are organically grown and free from pesticides and other harmful chemical additives.
5. The caloric content of a daily diet is adjusted to gain, maintain, or lose body weight, depending on which effect is desired.

Slimming Diets

Women throughout history have seldom been forced to diet to attain the type of slim figure currently in vogue. With few exceptions, the feminine ideal was a woman with a full, robust-looking figure. There have been only a few societies, and then only during short periods, that placed a premium on slimness in women.

The history of weight-loss dieting is an interesting one. The earliest recorded form of weight-loss dieting consisted of self-induced vomiting among women in ancient Rome. The *vomitorium,* an anteroom with special plumbing, was located adjacent to the dining area in all fashionable Roman homes. Originally the vomitorium was used by Roman men during periods of heavy feasting. They would simply eat until stuffed, hobble off to the *vomitorium,* stick fingers down their throats, empty their stomachs, and then return to the feast with renewed ability to taste the delicacies of the day.

No doubt, a matronly Roman woman took a cue from her husband and used the vomitorium to limit the number of calories that her body absorbed each day, while still being able to eat in a grand manner. It is an effective—albeit unpleasant—method of "dieting." L. M. Vincent, MD, indicates in his fine and interesting book, *Competing with the Sylph,* that self-induced vomiting is still a popular method of weight control among modern ballerinas!

Later in history fasting became the accepted method of weight control. Initially fasting was used for spiritual purposes, but it didn't take women long to discover that fasting also reduced their body fat levels. Fasting in various forms is still used by women to lose body weight. It's a quick and effective method of losing body fat, though not as pleasant a method as merely following a low-calorie diet.

The next development in weight-loss dieting was a crude form of low-calorie eating. Since food-calorie booklets are a relatively modern innovation, women at the turn of the 20th century weren't aware that fish was a food much lower in caloric content than beef. All they could do was lower their daily caloric intake by reducing the quantity of each food that they ate. It was a crude, but nonetheless effective, method of dieting to lose weight.

With the advent of calorie tables, the low-calorie diet became more and more refined until it reached the level of effectiveness described later in this chapter. Today a woman can merely eliminate high-fat foods from her diet, which drastically reduces caloric consumption, since one gram of fat yields nine calories when metabolized in the human body, while one gram of protein or carbohydrate yields only four calories. The modern low-calorie diet is also a very healthy form of eating, since it can be well-balanced nutritionally.

During the 1970s the low-carbohydrate diet was extremely popular. It remains a popular form of weight-reduction dieting, though its popularity is waning in comparison to the low-calorie form of weight-loss dieting. The low-carbohydrate diet is effective, but it is so nutritionally unbalanced that it can actually be harmful to your body if followed for long periods of time. Therefore, a continued decline in the popularity of the low-carbohydrate diet is expected.

goal of becoming slimmer and more physically attractive. It will always be too easy to say, "Hey, I look fine, so it won't hurt if I pig out on pizza and a hot fudge sundae *just this one time!*"

Slimming Techniques

Effective body slimming requires a combination of weight-loss dieting, regular exercise, and a changed self-image. Strangely, most obese men and women—and I was *definitely* a very obese young woman until the age of 20—don't actually visualize themselves as being fat. Even when I was 40–50 pounds overweight, for example, I thought of myself as still being as slim as I'd been at the age of nine or ten, at which point I had begun to grow obese from systematic overeating.

In the next chapter you will learn how to develop a positive mental approach to life, but let's briefly and specifically talk about image changing in relation to a slimming program. You *must* be confronted with what you really look like, or it will be almost impossible to stick to a weight-loss diet and exercise program. Without this self-confrontation you will never reach your

The key to changing a typical obese woman's self-image is to have her recognize and accept the fact that she *is* fat and that she *does* look terrible to most people. And the best way to accomplish this is to have a set of photographs taken of yourself in a bikini, standing with the front, side, and back of your body toward the camera. Or, if you really want to hit yourself between the eyes with the fact that you look like a pig, have the photos taken of yourself nude!

Enlarge each photo to 8 × 10. Then tape two or three on your bathroom or vanity mirror, on your refrigerator door, and anywhere else where you will see them regularly. When you look at these photographs every day, really *look* at them. Take note of every bulge and every square inch of cellulite, because these photos show *exactly* how you look.

Constantly seeing yourself graphically depicted as overweight will quickly help your attitude toward yourself and your self-image will become more realistic. Then you won't be able to kid yourself into thinking you really look good. And you will find that the photos, particularly the ones on your refrigerator door, will constantly reinforce your resolve to stay on a slimming diet!

Once you have lost a significant amount of weight, it's important to have a new set of photographs taken. Put them up next to the original photos, and you will see a considerable difference. *Convince* yourself that it was only through disciplined dieting and regular exercise that you were able to make such strides and that only by studiously applying these two factors for a longer period of time will you continue to make such significant progress. This way, the old photos–new photos combination will do wonders to reaffirm your resolve to continue with your slimming program.

The best slimming formula—once you have accepted a realistic image of yourself—is to combine a fat-loss diet with moderate daily exercise, particularly with aerobic activity (see Chapter 4 for a full discussion of aerobic activity and other forms of exercise). There are two basic types of weight-reduction diets, as well as two popular eating philosophies that are very conducive to loss of body fat. In the next few pages of this chapter we will explore each of these four nutritional philosophies for weight reduction, pointing out the strengths and weaknesses of each philosophy.

Low-Fat/Low-Calorie Dieting

In every human body there is a dynamic flow of energy (in the form of calories derived from the food you eat) into and out of the system. When an excess number of calories is taken in, your body stores them as fat at a rate of one pound for every 3,500 excess calories. And as a result of systematic overeating—as well as decreased physical activity levels as they grow older—many women are not as slim as they once were.

The way many women choose to lose excess body fat is to reverse the caloric balance to the point where they are taking in *fewer* calories than their bodies need to maintain a particular body weight. This is done by first calculating the number of calories the body needs for normal metabolism and daily physical activity. Then a diet is formulated to result in a total food intake each day of 500–750 calories less than the body's maintenance level. Such a diet will result in a loss of 1–1½ pounds of body fat each week, a very safe rate of weight loss.

To calculate your body's caloric maintenance level, assume that a normally active woman will need to consume 20–25 calories per pound of body weight to maintain her weight. (The figures for men are 25–30 calories per pound of body weight, should you be trying to help the man in your life reduce his own body fat levels.) Therefore, a normally active 110-pound woman will need to eat 2,200–2,750 calories per day to maintain her body weight.

With increased daily exercise, this caloric maintenance level will increase by 250–400 calories for each hour of training. And that is the primary reason that it is best to combine regular daily exercise with a good weight-reduction diet when slimming. A secondary reason that exercise is good for you when dieting is that it helps to maintain good skin tone and tightness as fat melts away from your body.

The caloric maintenance level we have calculated here is an average that will apply only to average women. A few women will have much higher maintenance levels, and they can easily be recognized. They are invariably slim and fat-free, and often they can maintain a fashion model's figure while actually eating ice cream and pizza every day!

I personally fall well below this average maintenance level. A great many women join me in this "low metabolic rate" group. Even on a 1,200-calorie-per-day diet, we may not lose weight, and on 2,000 calories per day we fatten up very quickly.

If you are in my metabolic group, you will know exactly how discouraging it has been over the years for me to lose weight. With my slow metabolism, I have to be doubly motivated, exercise twice as much, and be superhumanly dedicated to maintaining a strict diet. And I've had to do all of this just to lose a half pound of fat per week. It's been pure agony at times for me to lose weight, but the results have been well worth the struggle in the long run.

If you are on a 1,500-calorie-per-day diet and your fat levels are not dropping, you will need to gradually lower your daily caloric intake in increments of 100–200 calories per day each week until you *do* begin to lose weight. Weigh yourself every morning, and once you finally notice a downward weight trend, you will have found the caloric point at which you are in a weight-losing balance. If this level is only 700–750 calories per day, it will be difficult for you to stay on your diet, but when you do stay on it you will steadily lose body fat!

The trick to being able to maintain a low-calorie diet is to choose foods low in fat content. As mentioned earlier, each gram of fat yields nine calories of energy when metabolized in the human body, while both protein and carbohydrates yield only four calories. So, since fats are more than twice as concentrated in energy as proteins and carbohydrates, it makes sense to strictly limit fat intake when on a low-calorie diet.

By looking through the calorie chart in the second appendix of this book, you will quickly decide to reduce your consumption of such fatty foods as beef, pork, eggs, full-fat milk products, nuts and seeds, butter, oils, corn, margarine, and ice cream. But you *can* eat such tasty low-fat foods as fresh fruit, vegetables, fish, chicken, turkey, low-calorie breads, nonfat milk products, certain soups, unbuttered popcorn, and low-fat crackers. Be sure, however, when you cook

poultry to remove the skin, which is very fatty. Also, you should eat the white meat of chicken or turkey in preference to dark meat, which is higher in fat content.

By judiciously choosing what you eat on a low-calorie diet, you can consume rather large amounts of food and still keep your daily caloric intake quite low. As an example, you would have to eat *three pounds* of broiled fish to equal the caloric content of one pound of steak!

Utilizing the low-fat/low-calorie eating philosophy, here is a three-meal menu for one day:

Breakfast—bran cereal with nonfat milk, honey, fruit, slice of whole-grain toast, cup of black coffee or tea
Lunch—tuna salad with a minimum of mayonnaise, iced tea with honey, fruit
Dinner—broiled chicken breast, green beans, baked potato (without butter or sour cream), green salad (with vinegar for dressing), fruit, glass of nonfat milk

This particular menu—depending on the size of food portions consumed—would include between 1,200 and 1,500 calories for one day, even if you snacked on a couple of extra pieces of fresh fruit. And because the diet can be nutritionally well balanced, low-fat/low-calorie eating is a very healthy way to diet for fat reduction.

To conclude this section on low-fat/low-calorie eating, here are nine eating and cooking tips you can follow when using the diet:

1. If you can make a choice between pork and beef for a meal, choose beef, which is lower in caloric content. Similarly, choose chicken or turkey over beef, and fish over poultry.
2. Fry no foods, because fried food soaks up cooking oil like a sponge, drastically increasing a food's caloric content. Bake or broil fish and poultry. Charcoal

broiling is especially good, since it adds to the flavor of any food.

3. Cook with herbs and spices as often as you can, since each herb or spice will make a food a taste treat.

4. Never use commercial salad dressings or oil and vinegar dressing, since both contan high-calorie vegetable oils. Instead, sprinkle herbs over the salad, squeeze lemon juice on it, and then pour 2–3 tablespoons of apple cider vinegar over the salad. This combination makes a very taste-pleasing salad dressing.

5. Never boil vegetables, since boiling removes many of the foods' nutrients. Instead, lightly steam vegetables or eat them raw. It should go without saying that you should NEVER add butter to cooked vegetables.

6. Avoid dietary sodium, such as that contained in common table salt, diet sodas, and celery. One gram of sodium will retain 50 grams of water in your body, making you appear to have much more fat on your body than you actually have.

7. When using milk or milk products, use only nonfat milk and nonfat milk products. Of all hard cheeses, only mozzarella cheese is usually made from nonfat milk.

8. Use only high-fiber, whole-grain cereals and breads. Bread should be baked without added oil, butter, or shortening. Try to eat your bread without such toppings as peanut butter, jam, and jelly. Such tasty bread spreads can be three to four times as high in calories as a slice of plain, natural, whole-grain bread!

9. On almost any diet, you will have occasional sugar cravings. When you begin to crave sugar on a low-fat/low-calorie diet, a slice of watermelon or a peach will almost always satisfy such cravings without doing any caloric damage to your body.

Low-Carbohydrate Dieting

The low-carbohydrate diet reached its peak of popularity during the 1970s. The diet's ultimate popularity was fueled by several books on it written by physicians. The public always has confidence in physicians, so the diet was widely accepted. It also became quite popular because it resulted in a quick initial weight loss of five to ten pounds in only one week.

This diet is diametrically opposed to the low-fat diet, because it advocates high-protein/high-fat eating, which amounts to a very high-calorie diet. But the theory is that calories from fats aren't "fixed" in the body as fat deposits if the diet is devoid of, or very low in, carbohydrates.

If you buy a carbohydrate counter booklet at a drugstore, you will find that zero-carbohydrate foods include beef, pork, ham, bacon, fish, chicken, turkey, eggs, and cheese. Even butter, which is almost pure fat, is allowed to be eaten on this particular diet, as long as carbohydrates are kept out of the overall diet.

Carbohydrate foods include anything with flour or sugar in it, such as bread, cakes, cookies, soft drinks, ice cream, and candies. Other carbohydrate foods forbidden in the low-carb diet are milk, fruit, most vegetables, potatoes, and grains, all of which can be eaten on a low-calorie diet.

The low-carbohydrate diet does work well, particularly in terms of ridding the body of water, which causes a quick and dramatic weight loss. One gram of carbohydrate holds four grams of water in the human body, so when the body is virtually starved for carbohydrates it can't hold its usual amount of water. Once the water has been thrown off by your body, however, weight comes off rather slowly on a low-carbohydrate diet.

To use the low-carb diet effectively, plan to eat less than 30–50 grams of carbohydrate per day. Here is a typical daily eating schedule on the low-carb diet:

Breakfast—eggs, bacon, coffee with artificial sweetener and cream
Lunch—steak, green salad with Roquefort dressing, diet soda
Dinner—grilled pork chops, green beans, salad, cheese, iced tea with artificial sweetener
Snacks—cheese, cold cuts, hard-boiled eggs

While low-carbohydrate diets result in losses in body fat, they are not as healthy for most women as are low-fat/low-calorie diets. The human body, particularly the brain, needs a fairly large amount of carbohydrate to function properly. Most women following a low-carbohydrate diet will feel low in energy, think sluggishly, become prone to emotional depression, and tend to be very irritable. Keep these health hazards in mind when deciding whether or not to follow a low-carbohydrate diet.

Vegetarian Dieting

One of the easiest ways to lose weight and slim down is to adopt a vegetarian (excluding from the diet all animal products) or lacto-vegetarian (excluding all animal products except milk from the diet) eating philosophy. Avoiding all animal fats except those in milk products (or in eggs, as in a lacto-ovo-vegetarian diet) automatically makes your daily diet quite low in calories. And this makes the various vegetarian diets very similar in effect to the low-fat/low-calorie diet. Here is a typical lacto-vegetarian diet that you can try:

Breakfast—whole-grain cereal with nonfat raw milk and honey, fruit, herbal tea
Lunch—large green salad with sunflower seeds and a wide variety of vegetables and seed sprouts, glass of nonfat raw milk
Dinner—cheese and vegetable casserole, small green salad, baked potato, raw vegetables, nonfat raw milk
Snacks—fruit, raw vegetables, cheese, nuts, seeds, yogurt, cottage cheese

Anyone who has been a vegetarian for at least six months is almost guaranteed not to be fat.

Fasting

As mentioned earlier, fasting is one of the oldest methods of dieting for weight loss. There are three basic types of fasts:

1. A pure water fast, in which only water is consumed for several days
2. A juice fast, in which only fruit and vegetable juices are consumed for several days
3. A protein drink fast, in which only liquid amino acids, or concentrated protein powder mixed in water, are consumed for several days

A pure water fast is the most difficult to maintain, at least for the first two or three days. In all forms of fasting, a condition called *autolysis* is reached after two to four days. *Autolysis* means literally "self-eating," and in a state of autolysis the human body actually begins to feed on itself to supply its energy and tissue repair needs.

When a state of autolysis has been reached, the body consumes its tissues selectively, using the least vital tissues (fat, tumors, dead cells, etc.) first. Later the body begins to consume its own skeletal muscles. It is only after prolonged fasting that the body begins to use such vital tissues as the heart, nerves, eyes, and liver. At that point, death is very close.

A pure water fast for three to five days will result in a considerable weight loss, much of it in body fat. You will, however, feel quite weak and uncomfortable on such a fast. You will undoubtedly find a juice fast more comfortable, because you can drink all of the fresh fruit and vegetable juices you would like to consume. This keeps your energy levels up and feelings of hunger to a minimum, but the body still reaches autolysis after about three days of juice fasting. You'll probably be able to juice fast comfortably for three to seven days the first time you try it and for even longer periods of time once you are used to this type of fast.

Both a pure water fast and a juice fast should be broken gradually, over a period of two to three days. Eat only fruit and perhaps a slice of whole-grain bread the first day. Add a little solid protein food, more fruit, and a salad the second day, and then even more food the third day. By the third or fourth day you should again be eating normally.

Moving from a fast immediately to normal eating can cause you to binge. And such binge eating will cause severe diarrhea. It's much easier and healthier to move gradually from fasting to normal eating over a period of two to three days.

The final type of fast—drinking liquid protein—was in vogue for about a year during the mid-1970s. But it appears that liquid protein fasting is very dangerous. Several women developed heart irregularities on this fast and died, whereupon the Food and Drug Administration (FDA) began to campaign against liquid protein fasting. As a result, I certainly do not recommend that you use this type of weight-loss regimen.

All fasts should be supervised by a physician or a naturopathic doctor who is experienced in conducting fasts. Under such conditions, fasting can be very safe and can result in significant body fat losses.

Weight-Gain Dieting

Through my personal appearances and health and fitness seminars with my husband Lou, I have discovered that a significant number of women are plagued by the inability to gain weight. To them, being very thin is just as traumatic as being very fat is to an obese woman.

Fortunately, this problem can be solved by combining the weight-gain diet in this section with a heavy weight training program aimed toward weight gain. Such a weight-gain workout is outlined in Chapter 4. By following a combined diet and exercise program, you can gain one or two pounds of solid body weight each month until you have reached a more normal body weight.

Nutritionally, the key to gaining body weight is to increase the body's ability to digest and assimilate protein. This, in combination with heavy weight training, adds to the growth of the body's muscle mass and consequently to a woman's solid body weight. You need not worry about appearing masculine from the weight training, however, because your naturally high levels of the hormone estrogen will cause added muscle mass to appear on your body as feminine curves.

A woman's digestive system can process only about 20–25 grams of protein for use each time she eats. Therefore, the idea of eating two or three large meals per day is self-defeating to an overly thin woman, because only 20–25 percent of a 100-gram protein meal can be used by the body. Most of the rest of the protein is simply excreted from the body and therefore is wasted for weight gain.

The logical way to increase the body's total daily protein absorption is to eat four to six smaller, protein-rich meals each day. This is basically a matter of snacking all day long, because such frequent meals must be kept small. Typically, you can eat a six-ounce serving of fish or a three-egg cheese omelette at each meal for your protein intake.

For some underweight women, even eating six meals per day will not help. In such cases, the problem is usually inefficient digestion. Some women's digestive systems simply don't produce enough digestive acids and enzymes to process nutrients in the stomach properly. If this is your problem, you should supplement each meal with hydrochloric acid tablets and/or digestive enzymes (papain, the enzyme found in pineapple, is one of the best digestive enzymes).

Both hydrochloric acid and digestive enzymes can be purchased in health food stores. Simply follow label instructions, and soon your digestive efficiency will be up to normal functioning. Often this will help you begin to gain weight more quickly.

One final nondietary weight-gain tip is *keep a tranquil mind.* Being constantly nervous and uptight about things beyond your control will burn up tremendous quantities of energy that could add body weight to your slender frame instead. So, keep calm and get plenty of sleep, and you'll find that rest and energy conservation will improve the rate at which you can gain body weight.

Regardless of how well you eat and how faithfully you train, weight gains will come slowly. But Rome wasn't built in a day, and you should take solace in the philosophy that nothing worth having will ever come easily to you. Work hard for a good weight gain, and you will gradually achieve it!

Organic Eating

The object of organic eating, which grows more popular every year, is to eliminate or reduce the "body pollution" caused by processed, pesticide-sprayed, or otherwise chemically treated foods in the human diet. Even when you wash foods thoroughly, these chemicals can cling to what you eat and enter your body. And this body pollution can cause a wide variety of ill effects.

The best way to assure yourself of organically grown or raised food is to grow or raise it yourself. Unfortunately, this is impractical for city dwellers. We who live in metropolitan areas must depend on health food stores and organic produce stores for our organic fruits, vegetables, and meats.

I strongly recommend that you prepare and consume organically grown foods whenever possible. Eliminate harmful toxins from your body, and you will contribute considerably to increased longevity and overall health. Even small amounts of pesticides can be concentrated in the human body over a period of years, until a toxic level of the chemical has been reached, causing illness and even death.

Judging Food Quality

Good quality food is a prerequisite to cooking nutritionally healthy meals. Therefore, you should know how to judge foods and pick those of the best quality when shopping. Here are ten good food-buying rules:

1. **Read dates of expiration.** Every perishable food, such as milk, eggs, and cheese, must now have an expiration date stamped on its package. If you buy and use such foods before the expiration date and store the foods appropriately, they will be fresh when used.

2. **Try to buy organically grown foods.** As discussed earlier, organic produce and other foods are available in most large health food stores as well as in some markets. Organic foods are guaranteed to be grown in clean, chemical-free soil without the use of pesticides. So, by using predominantly organic foods in your cooking, you avoid chemical body pollution.

3. **Try to avoid canned and frozen foods.** Most canned foods are loaded with preservatives, and large amounts of salt and/or sugar have been added to them. Frozen foods oxidize rapidly when thawed, and they end up having much less nutritional value than fresh foods. Surprisingly, many so-called "fresh" foods (such as eggs and meat) have been frozen while being transported cross-country, then thawed before being sold.

4. **Check the color of fish flesh.** If a white-fleshed fish has turned pink, or a pink-fleshed fish looks a deeper shade of pink than usual, this indicates that the fish wasn't cleaned until long after it was caught. The pinkness is caused by blood and other impurities slowly seeping into the flesh, and the color is a tip-off that the fish isn't as fresh as it should be.

5. **Check the color and texture of beef.** While Lou and I seldom eat beef, due to its high fat content, you may eat it, so you should know how to buy the best quality of meat. Correctly aged beef is purplish-brown when first cut, and it changes quickly to a bright red as oxygen reaches the cut surface of the meat. Look for bright red-colored meat when you are buying fresh beef. The fat in good beef should be white, and it should flake off easily with a fork.

6. **Note the color and texture of pork.** As with beef, fresh pork has a characteristic color and fat texture. The meat should be a pale grayish-pink color. The fat should be white, firm to the touch, and free from fibers.

7. **Check the appearance of poultry.** Both chicken and turkey, which Lou and I eat in large quantities, should have soft, smooth-feeling meat. The fat of a chicken should be distributed evenly beneath its skin. The skin of good-quality chicken should be unblemished and moist, and if the chicken is fresh, the breastbone will be pliable and not brittle.

8. **Choose fresh-looking fruits and vegetables.** Fruit can be judged by feel, color, and smell. Ripe fruit smells like ripe fruit, and all ripe fruits should be firmly soft but not mushy. Cantaloupe should have no green surface area, particularly along the ribs. Both cantaloupe and honeydew melon will have a shifting mass of seeds inside when the fruit is shaken, IF they are ripe. The stem of a watermelon should be dry and hard, not green, and the melon should sound firm when rapped with the knuckles.

   In general, fresh vegetables will be crisp and firm feeling, and no wilting will be evident. When choosing lettuce, get the heaviest head, as long as there is no wilting or browning evident. Heavy heads have more layers of leaves and are thus a better value when you pay a set price per head of lettuce.

9. **Some foods must be aged for highest quality.** Cheeses, wines, and other foods are of better quality when they have been aged. You should note both how long a food has been aged and its product expiration date.

10. **Read all labels.** The ingredients of all packaged foods must be listed on the label, with the ingredient used in the largest proportion listed first. By scrutinizing every food label, you can find hidden sugar, sodium, and preservatives in foods and then avoid these foods in your diet. As an example, my husband Lou is of Italian heritage, and he loves eating salami. Unfortunately, though, he can eat only homemade salamis, because the commercial versions are loaded with both sugar and sodium.

Low-Sodium Eating

A low-sodium diet is often associated with persons who suffer from high blood pressure and heart disease. When such problems become apparent, the patient is told by his or her physician to limit intake of table salt and other foods containing sodium. Cutting sodium out of your diet limits water retention in the body, which in turn lowers blood pressure.

Low-sodium eating is also a good idea for perfectly healthy men and women. One gram of excess sodium in your body (and your body needs very little sodium to function well) will retain nearly 50 grams of water, since sodium has a tremendous affinity for water. In women water retention can be unsightly, and it is unhealthy for all human beings.

By limiting your sodium intake, you can look better, feel better, and live longer. The most obvious way to do this is to stop using table salt in cooking, replacing it with other (sodium-free) herbs and spices. You'll also need to reduce or eliminate from your diet all foods containing preservatives (e.g., bacon, potato chips, canned and packaged foods, etc.). Virtually all food preservatives contain sodium, as do artificial sweeteners, which are made from sodium saccharide.

Numerous cookbooks are available with recipes for low-sodium cooking, some offering low-sodium recipes exclusively. These can be found in bookstores as well as in health food stores. One of the best of these books is *The American Health Association Cookbook*. Health and nutrition magazines such as *Prevention* also regularly carry low-sodium recipes. So why not try low-sodium eating? It can be just as delicious as eating salted food, and it's much healthier!

Food Supplementation

Regardless of how carefully you choose foods and prepare your meals, it is still possible to develop nutritional deficiencies, particularly of vitamins and minerals. To be sure that neither Lou nor I develops such deficiencies, we supplement our meals with vitamins and minerals in tablet and capsule form. As far as we are concerned, these concentrated nutrients are inexpensive health insurance.

While I don't advocate megavitamin therapy, you shouldn't be afraid to use rather high dosages of vitamins and minerals. Except for oil-soluble vitamins—A, D, E, and K—it is impossible to consume too much of either vitamins or minerals. The excess nutrients are merely excreted through the urine or feces. Oil-soluble vitamins, however, are stored in the body and could reach toxic levels with long-term overusage.

Each woman should individualize her supplementation schedule, taking some type of supplement with each meal. Later in this section, a chart of commonly used vitamins and minerals is presented, from which you can choose the vitamin and mineral tablets and capsules for your own personal supplementation program.

Try a particular supplement for two or three weeks, noting its effects on your energy levels, mental alertness, the way your body feels, and so on. Several months of such experiments, during which you constantly note the biofeedback your body gives you, will allow you to formulate a supplementation program geared specifically to the needs of your unique body.

To begin with, take a multiple vitamin-mineral tablet with each meal. This will provide your body with basic nutritional insurance, and from this starting point you can gradually add individual nutrients. Try the following supplements in this order:

1. vitamin C
2. vitamin B complex
3. chelated multiple minerals
4. vitamin E
5. chelated calcium
6. chelated iron

All of the minerals you take in supplement form should be chelated. Chelation is a process in which protein molecules are chemically bonded to the mineral molecules,

Food Supplement Chart

Supplement	Effects on Body
Multiple Vitamins-Minerals	Provide a wide spectrum of nutrients needed by the human body.
Vitamin C	Necessary for effecient tissue repair; helps prevent colds and infections; detoxifies body.
Vitamin B complex	Promotes healthy nerve function, good appetite and overall physical and mental well-being; helps form enzymes in the human body.
Chelated Multiple Minerals	Essential in most of the body's physiological processes, especially in fat metabolism and energy production.
Vitamin E	Works as an antioxidant against air and water pollution; necessary to normal function of heart and blood vessels; necessary for normal sexual function.
Calcium	Builds and repairs teeth and bones; calms the nerves.
Iron	Essential in forming red blood cells; particularly essential to women who are menstruating.
Magnesium	Essential in all subcellular metabolic activity; promotes healthy joints and connective tissues.
Trace Elements (Potassium, Sodium, Copper, Iodine, Zinc, Manganese)	Only small traces of each are evident in the human body, but an absence of any one trace element can cause severe chemical disturbances; kelp tablets are an excellent source of trace elements.
Vitamin A	Important in the young for proper growth and maturation; needed for clear, healthy skin; essential to eye health.
Vitamin D	Essential for pregnant and nursing women; forms strong teeth and bones.
Food Enzymes	Available in most raw foods, particularly fresh fruits, and easily destroyed by heat; enzymes are the chemical catalysts of the body's biological processes.

Daily Supplements

Supplement	Daily Amount
Multiple Vitamins-Minerals	3-6 capsules
Vitamin C	1,000-3,000 mg
Vitamin B Complex (high potency)	3-6 capsules
Chelated Multiple Minerals	3-6 tablets
Vitamin E	400-1,200 IU
Calcium	1,000-2,000 mg
Iron	100-300 mg
Magnesium	1-3 tablets
Kelp	10-20 tablets
Dessicated Liver	10-20 tablets
Vitamin A	5,000-10,000 IU
Vitamin D	400-1,200 USP units
Digestive Enzymes	1-2 tablets (each meal)

making the minerals more absorbable by the human body.

In order to assess accurately the impact of various nutrients on your body, take a look at the chart of commonly used food supplements on page 16.

To be sure that my body gets all of the nutrients just discussed, I take one high-potency multiple vitamin-mineral capsule with each meal. For proper absorption, you should always take your vitamins and minerals with meals.

Some women are interested in the megavitamin approach to food supplementation, and my husband follows such a philosophy when he is training particularly hard. If you want to be *totally* sure that you are taking in enough vitamins and minerals for super health, take the nutrients on above chart every day, dividing them up equally for consumption with each meal.

The Cytotoxic Diet

One of the most remarkable nutritional philosophies developed in recent years is that behind the cytotoxic diet, which results in great weight loss as well as drastically improved health. This diet involves taking a blood test to determine a woman's food allergies and then cutting those allergenic foods out of the diet.

Everyone has heard of food allergies. Aunt Maude eats strawberries and breaks out in hives 30 minutes later, or Cousin Jack eats milk products and comes down with asthma within the hour. But the food allergies considered by the cytotoxic diet are not quite so dramatic. Rather, they are low-level food allergies that have adverse effects on the body over long periods of time.

What can these allergies do to your body? Their effects can be both wide-reaching and catastrophic. Here is a comprehensive list of food allergy effects adapted from *Tracking Down Hidden Food Allergy* by William G. Crook, MD:

Physical Symptoms

Head: Headaches, faintness, dizziness, feeling of fullness in the head, excessive drowsiness or sleepiness soon after eating, insomnia.

Eyes, Ears, Nose, and Throat: Runny nose, stuffy nose, excessive formation of mucus, watery eyes, blurred vision, ringing of the ears, earache, fullness in the ears, fluid in the middle ear, hearing loss, recurrent ear infections, itching ear, ear drainage, sore throat, chronic cough, gagging, canker sores, itching of the roof of the mouth, recurrent sinusitis.

Heart and Lungs: Palpitations, increased

heart rate, rapid heart rate (tachycardia), asthma, chest congestion, hoarseness.

Gastrointestinal System: Nausea, vomiting, diarrhea, constipation, bloating after meals, belching, colitis, flatulence (passing gas), feeling of fullness in the stomach long after finishing a meal, abdominal pains or cramps.

Skin: Hives, rashes, eczema, dermatitis, skin pallor, acne.

Other Physical Symptoms: Chronic fatigue, weakness, muscle aches and pains, joint aches and pains, swelling of the hands, swelling of the feet, swelling of the ankles, urinary tract symptoms (frequency, urgency), vaginal itching, vaginal discharge, hunger (and its close ally; binge or spree eating).

Psychological Symptoms: Anxiety, "panic attacks," depression, "crying jags," aggressive behavior, irritability, mental dullness, mental lethargy, confusion, excessive daydreaming, hyperactivity, restlessness, learning disabilities, poor work habits, slurred speech, stuttering, inability to concentrate, indifference.

Remarkable cures resulting from the cytotoxic diet have been recorded. A friend of mine was completely cured of severe arthritis in his hands, insomnia, acne, chronic headaches, swollen glands, chronic fatigue, anxiety, depression, aggressive behavior, and inability to concentrate after less than a month on the cytotoxic diet.

He found that of the 160 foods for which he was tested, he was allergic to 40 foods (the average person is allergic to approximately 20 percent of the foods for which he or she is tested). As my friend noted recently, "The allergy test is almost foolproof. A small blood sample is drawn and then centrifuged to remove the plasma and white blood cells. Then tiny drops of white blood cells are put on microscope slides with each of 160 food concentrates. After two hours the slides are examined under the microscope. If the body is not allergic to a food,

the white blood cells will remain normal. But if there is an allergic reaction, the blood cells will become structurally changed, or—in the case of a severe food allergy—the cell walls will rupture."

Numerous allergists around America give this test, and you can call your state medical association for the names of physicians in your area who are experienced with the cytotoxic diet.

Dr. James Braly, head of the Optimum Health Labs, Encino, California, has written about the cytotoxic diet in numerous magazine articles. As he has explained,

We recommend that patients eat nonoffending foods rotationally, repeating a particular food in the diet no more often than every four days. This helps prevent food allergies, which often develop from simply eating a food too frequently. It also induces a patient to eat a wider variety of foods. The average American eats only about 15 different foods over and over again. I prefer to see my patients eating two to three times that number, which automatically gives them a healthier and better-balanced diet.

Most patients are allergic to the foods that they eat most frequently. This is because allergenic foods cause an actual addiction, and your body begins to crave those foods. So, if you're allergic to sucrose, common white sugar, you'll feel temporarily better when you're eating a lot of sugar-laden foods.

To illustrate how a food addiction works, let's examine how smoking tobacco becomes an addiction, because the cases are identical. Few people who ever began smoking cigarettes liked the taste of tobacco or the body's reaction to the first few cigarettes. But the nicotine in tobacco is a powerful poison, and the body's defense systems are forced into high gear to fight off the toxins. Thus, for a few minutes after smoking a cigarette, a smoker feels a physical and mental boost.

The same thing happens when you eat an allergenic food. The food is toxic to your body, and it causes the body's defense mechanisms to swing into action. And you feel a definite boost. But, unfortunately, these toxins have long-range harmful effects on the human body.

Food allergies are most often manifested in the body as inflammations, which is why arthritis is a common by-product of food allergies. And since inflammations hold a great deal of water in the body, a person can look bloated—even fat—if he or she eats a lot of allergenic foods.

The key to successfully following the cytotoxic diet is eating simply. Since you won't know for sure what ingredients are in most restaurant dishes, you'll have to eat mostly at home and primarily basic, simple meals. Something like beef stroganoff or macaroni and cheese will be virtually impossible to eat because of the wide range of ingredients in each of these dishes.

If a man or woman can stay strictly on a cytotoxic diet for three to four months, most of his or her food allergies will have been eliminated. After three months you can reintroduce each of the allergenic foods into your diet, one at a time, noting what allergy symptoms they induce. Usually they won't cause any problems. If that is the case, you can include them rotationally in your overall diet.

Within a few weeks of eliminating the allergenic foods from your diet, you'll notice some drastic changes in your physical and psychological well-being. One immediate result is a marked weight loss. Some patients lose up to 10–15 pounds in two or three weeks. This is primarily water that is flushed from the system once the allergy-induced inflammations have abated.

Virtually all allergy-induced physical and psychological symptoms will be eliminated after four to six weeks on the cytotoxic diet.

The cytotoxic test is rather expensive—$250–$350 on an average, including the accompanying consultations—but the results the diet gives in weight loss and health improvement are well worth the expense. Still, many women either don't have access to an allergist who can give them the test or they can't afford to take it. For these women, Dr. Braly offers some additional advice.

"Most people are allergic to milk products and/or grains," Dr. Braly said. "Even if you can't take the test, it would be a good idea to drop these two food groups from your diet for three months. If you do, you probably will notice a considerable improvement in your physical and mental health in only two or three weeks!"

Conclusion

By using the simple guidelines for optimum nutrition contained in this chapter, you will be able to formulate a daily nutritional schedule that will vastly improve your own health and that of your family. And when you possess good health, you have everything!

In Chapter 3 you will learn a unique mental approach to life that will give you both inner peace and the ability to use your mind power to its fullest extent to reach your health and fitness goals.

3

Mental Approach and Stress Reduction

The essence of a fitness and health minded woman's mental approach to life boils down to one word—*positive!* By concentrating on positive thinking and reinforcing this attitude through positive health and fitness experiences, you can feel good about yourself 24 hours a day. You can truly find mental tranquility.

Mental Approach

By adopting a good mental approach to life, you can also use your mind to motivate yourself, achieve your goals in life, and mentally program yourself for success. And all of these tremendous mental benefits can be achieved rather easily, simply by using the suggestions outlined in the balance of this chapter.

Positive Thinking

From my own unhappy teenage years, I know that it's easy to dwell on the negative aspects of life. When I couldn't get a date, for example, I was depressed for days. And

instead of concentrating my thoughts on the positive aspects of my life (e.g., my intelligence and good grades in school), all I could think about was the negative aspects (my obesity and my low energy levels).

Merely by making up your mind to think positively as often as possible throughout the day, you can drastically improve your sense of well-being. And by combining a good diet and regular exercise with positive thinking, you can make consistent progress in your physical fitness and personal appearance that gradually reinforces your positive thought process. Success breeds success, until you suddenly find your life completely changed. I know this implicitly, because it happened just this way in my case.

To initiate the positive thinking process, compile a list of things you like and dislike about yourself. Then try to think every day about the positive things on your list, totally ignoring the entries in the negative column. Almost automatically, you will find yourself thinking less and less about the negative parts of your life, and eventually your thinking will be almost 100 percent positive!

Motivation

In order to stick to a program of regular exercise and a healthy diet—and to start such programs in the first place—it is necessary to develop, and then maintain, a high level of personal motivation. In the long run, success feeds on motivation and motivation feeds on success.

To obtain motivation to train and diet, you must first find inspiration. The best form of inspiration for most women is simply making a firm decision to improve. In Chapter 2 we talked about having photos taken of yourself in a swimsuit and then constantly looking at those photos. Such a practice will also build great motivation to improve yourself.

Once you get your "inspiration ball" rolling, you'll find it easy to keep it rolling. With every compliment you receive ("You're *really* losing weight!") from a friend, it will roll a little faster. And soon the ball will be rolling so fast and with such great momentum that literally nothing will stop it.

An end result of inspiration and motivation is enthusiasm, which is the ingredient that actually keeps you exercising and dieting consistently for long periods of time. Enthusiasm also feeds on success and results in more success. Essentially,

MOTIVATION + INSPIRATION

+ ENTHUSIASM = SUCCESS

In addition to gaining motivation from the constant (albeit small) health, appearance, and fitness successes that come to me, I have discovered a couple of motivation-building methods, which I use consistently to maintain my own level of enthusiasm.

The first of these is to read biographies of famous people, as well as the success stories of women in *Muscle & Fitness, Shape,* and all the other health- and fitness-oriented magazines. I can easily identify with each of the women in these inspirational stories, because in one way or another I have walked the same path as has each of these successful women. And because I can identify so strongly with them, I share in these individuals' successes, which in turn significantly increases my enthusiasm and motivation.

The second method I use to maintain high levels of motivation is to keep a detailed record of my workouts and physical progress. I write down everything I do in my physical training and everything I eat, and I have photos taken of myself each month or two. With my diary I can easily look back a year in the book and see vividly in my notes and progress photos how much I have improved during the year. Seeing such improvement really peaks my motivation to continue progressing.

Goal Setting

The best way I have found to keep mentally focused on constantly improving myself is to set goals, achieve them, and then set newer and higher goals. These goals come in two types—long-range goals and intermediate, short-range goals set as stepping-stones between the long-range goals.

Long-range goals should be set yearly, and they should cover a lot of territory. At the same time, however, long-range goals should be realistically achievable. If you are 120 pounds overweight, it's not too realistic to expect to lose every pound of excess fat in only one year (an average of more than two pounds of fat loss each week). But shooting to lose 40 pounds—or less than one pound per week—is quite reasonable, and three years of such consistent losses will give you a total loss of 120 pounds.

The eminent Chinese philosopher Confucius noted, "The journey of a thousand miles is started with a single step." Of course, Confucius implied that there were a lot of single steps along the thousand-mile journey, in addition to the first one.

To corollate this proverb with goal setting, a thousand-mile journey is a long-range goal. The prospect of walking a thousand miles would be mind-boggling to anyone, but the idea of taking a single step, or even walking a mile, is comprehended and accomplished easily. So, to continue the analogy, the mile walk is a short-range goal.

Short-range goals can be established weekly or monthly, and they are parts of the yearly long-range goals. But with each part, as with each mile walked, the overall, long-range whole is approached. After having walked a thousand one-mile segments, you will have walked a full thousand miles.

Let's say that you have set a long-range goal of losing 50 pounds in one year (I actually had this goal one year, and I reached it quite comfortably). Breaking this down into weekly goals, you would be able to lose 52 pounds in a year if you lost only one pound each week. And losing a pound per week doesn't sound like much, does it?

As I mentioned earlier, the key to using goal setting is to achieve each goal and then set higher goals. After several years of routinely achieving goals and setting new ones, you will find that you have reached an exceptional level of health, physical appearance, and physical fitness!

When discussing my philosophy of self-motivation, I mentioned the importance of keeping a health and fitness diary. You'll also find that keeping such a diary ties in well with the goal-setting techniques just discussed.

Writing down your short-range and long-range goals in your diary gives you a graphic illustration of your progress toward each goal. While it's difficult to see progress from day to day, it's very easy to see it from month to month or year to year.

Visualization

My husband Lou recently taught me how to use visualization, a mental technique that has helped him enormously in his own competitive bodybuilding. And after using visualization for only a few weeks, I have concluded that it is a valuable technique for all improvement-minded women.

Visualization programs your subconscious mind to help you reach your goals. The subconscious mind is very powerful, and when you have convinced it of the

importance of some course of action, it helps you reach whatever goal you have set.

It's rather easy to program your subconscious mind. All you need to do is decide what goal you want to pursue and then consistently and regularly visualize yourself as having already achieved that goal. Of course, the goal that you use in the visualization process—as is the case with all goals—must be a realistic one, but visualization allows you to achieve it more easily than you could normally reach it.

To illustrate how to use visualization, let's assume that you wish to lose 20 pounds of body fat. Spend some time developing a strong mental image of how you will look and feel when you're 20 pounds lighter. Make this mental picture as vivid and realistic as possible. See the thinner face you'll have, the narrower hips, the slimmer thighs, the smaller dress size and nicer fashions you'll wear, even part of the new wardrobe you'll buy when you ultimately reach your goal.

Once you have developed a good mental "photograph" of the way you *will* soon look, concentrate on that image for 10–15 minutes one or two times per day. Do this whenever you can find a time that you can be fully relaxed and free from distractions, and be sure to visualize your new image every day.

I use visualization just before I fall asleep each night. Then I'm fully relaxed, and I can often fall asleep with the image still in my mind, which programs the subconscious mind even more strongly than normally. Try visualization in this manner, and you'll find yourself progressing toward your goals with surprising speed!

Mind Power!

The mind is the most powerful organ in the human body, and I strongly suggest that you use your mind to its fullest potential. Your mind controls, either consciously or subconsciously, every process and action your body undertakes. Master your mind, and you will reach every goal that you set.

Coping with Stress

Stress is all about us, and it affects every person to a certain degree. Essentially, stress is any force or pressure put on the human mind or body, and it can be either positive (such as receiving a job promotion) or negative (as in losing a much-needed job). As a general rule, however, stress is thought of as a set of negative forces placed on each of us by today's fast-paced, impersonal, high-pressure lifestyle. I've felt this stress, and I'm sure that you have, too.

Hans Selye, MD, PhD, founder and president of the International Institute of Stress, headquartered in Montreal, is considered the world's foremost authority on stress and its effect on the human mind and body. Dr. Selye wrote in a Blue Cross booklet called *Help Yourself!*

You should not and cannot avoid stress, because to eliminate it completely would mean to destroy life itself. If you make no more demands on your body, you are dead. Whatever you do—run up a flight of stairs, play tennis, worry, or fight starvation—demands are made on you. A lash of the whip and a passionate kiss can be equally stressful! Although one causes **distress** (bad stress), the other **eustress** (good stress), both make common demands, requiring you to adapt to a change from your normal equilibrium. Even when you sleep, your heart continues to beat, your lungs breathe, your stomach digests last night's meal, and even your brain continues to function: you dream. It is really quite unthinkable that anyone could, or would want to, avoid stress.

Both positive and negative stresses elicit a common endocrinological response from your body. In situations of extreme stress, the hypothalmus gland stimulates the pituitary gland to release the extremely potent hormone adrenalin. This hormone elevates the pulse rate and blood pressure, makes all of the body's senses hyperalert, shuts down those organ systems not immediately necessary to fight for survival, and makes the body's skeletal muscles many times stronger than they normally are. Thus, adrenalin prepares the body either to fight for its life or to flee hastily from danger. This is why adrenalin is called the "fight or flight hormone."

Ordinary everyday stress doesn't elicit such an extreme response from the body's endocrinological system, but it does elicit a definite, albeit small, response. Over the course of months and years, these minor stresses accumulate in the mind and body sufficiently to cause physical or mental illness. Dr. Selye theorizes that accumulated negative stress eventually causes the body's immunological systems to break down, thus leaving us open to diseases to which we wouldn't normally succumb.

If the body is exposed to prolonged and heavy negative stress, it can actually perish. This has been proven many times with laboratory animals. Ordinarily, however, a person's symptoms of overstress are far less catastrophic, though still a threat to health. Some of the more common symptoms of overstress include chronic nervousness, depression, irritability, anxiety, insomnia, tension-related headaches, chronic fatigue, frequent illness, drug dependence, sexual dysfunction, and poor concentration.

Should you suffer from such symptoms, you must determine which stressor agents are causing them and then attempt to remove them. Can you think of what is currently causing you stress? Here are some hints: rush-hour traffic, unrequited love, a burned meal, a fight with a spouse or co-worker, a car breakdown, unexpected bills, missing an airplane flight, gloomy weather, excessive noise, sudden loud noise.

You will most often be under pressure, and thus be stressed, in social situations, at work, or in your interpersonal relationships. For the next week or two, write down each instance of stress to which you are subjected and identify the probable stressor. With such a stress diary to refer to, you will soon see patterns developing. Certain situations and individuals will almost *always* cause you negative stress.

In many cases you can reduce your stress levels simply by avoiding your most common stressors. Indeed, this is the simplest stress-reduction method known to any woman. There are, however, stressors that can't be avoided easily—e.g., those on the job. In such cases you should seek to minimize your reaction to the stress.

The easiest way to reduce unavoidable stress—and, unfortunately, a method that millions of American women choose—is to resort to drugs. But in this case the easiest way is definitely not the best way; indeed, it is the worst possible way to combat stress. Valium tablets and Quaaludes are widely used in America. In fact, Valium is prescribed worldwide more frequently than any other drug!

I agree that Valium and Quaaludes do mask feelings of stress, just as does alcohol. But all three of these drugs are physically addictive, particularly Quaaludes. You can become physically addicted to Valium, as well, with daily use for as few as three weeks. And there are hundreds of thousands of closet alcoholics among our country's housewives. You would be wise never to use any of these harmful, self-destructive drugs.

Perhaps even more crucial than the addictive properties of such drugs is the fact that they frequently mask the serious symptoms of advanced stress breakdown. If you regularly take such drugs, your family physician might well be unable to determine that you are in an acute stage of stress-induced illness.

There are numerous natural (and safer)

ways to deal with stress than popping pills or taking a drink. One of the best of these is regular exercise, which is discussed thoroughly in Chapter 4. Nothing feels quite as good after a stressful day or dissipates stress as effectively as a hard workout. Individual exercise is fine in this case, but it's usually better in terms of stress reduction to compete in racquetball, squash, tennis, or some other type of head-to-head physical competition. I personally always feel *great* after a hard tennis match.

Dr. Thaddeus Kostrabala, a physician practicing in San Diego, has done considerable research on what he refers to as a "positive sports addiction." During strenuous exercise the brain releases a hormone called *endorphin,* which rapidly dissipates stress and causes a natural high. Some researchers have called endorphin a "natural opiate" for its mood-elevating properties. And, incidentally, you will feel no "crash" when the endorphin wears off, just a pleasant, long-lasting, stress-free, mellow sensation. I have often experienced this feeling, and it's unbeatable!

Hypnosis also has great potential for stress reduction, because it is nothing more than a deep state of relaxation into which stress can't intrude. Anytime you are fully relaxed you are virtually impervious to stress. And once you have been hypnotized two or three times, your hypnotist can give you posthypnotic suggestions that will allow you to use self-hypnosis to reduce daily stress levels. I've had hypnosis treatments myself, and they have yielded superb results.

Fractional body relaxation is a sort of homemade form of hypnosis, but nonetheless it's an effective way to combat stress. Begin using this technique by lying on your back in bed with a pillow under your knees and another under your head and neck. Place your arms in a relaxed position along the sides of your torso and slightly spread your legs. Close your eyes, but not too

tightly. Even your eyelids must be relaxed during this procedure.

Next concentrate on your breathing, taking four to six seconds to take in a deep breath slowly and another four to six seconds to expel it. Hold each full breath for a count of three before beginning to expel it. Breathe in and out slowly and rhythmically through both your mouth and nose like this for three to five minutes. By this point you should already be well on your way to being fully relaxed and free from stress.

Starting with your toes, and continuing your rhythmic breathing, think the tension out of every joint and muscle in your body. Firmly tell your right foot to relax, and it soon will. So will every other part of your body as you think about it, until about 20 minutes later your body will be so fully relaxed that you will feel as though you are floating on a cloud.

With practice, you will be able to relax your whole body in as few as 10 minutes. Once you are completely relaxed, lie in that state for five to ten minutes. And once you arise from your relaxed state, you will feel totally refreshed and free of stress-induced tension. You can practice this technique two or three times per day, whenever you feel particularly stressed.

Meditation is another form of relaxation that can help you abolish stress from your life. You can study transcendental meditation, zen meditation, mantra-repeating meditation, or focal-point meditation. Various schools and groups teach each of these forms of meditation. As with fractional relaxation, you can practice meditation two or three times per day, whenever you feel stressed. Many women have given enthusiastic reports on the effectiveness of meditation in reducing stress.

Adopting a hobby is another classic way to manage stress, and the range of hobbies from which you can choose is virtually unlimited. Physical hobbies are preferable, but sedentary hobbies—sewing, collecting coins or stamps, writing letters to your friends and relatives, etc.—can also be valuable in stress reduction. Simply pick the hobby that appeals to you most, which can be carried on comfortably within your financial means, and that will hold your interest for many years.

Finally, you can fight stress nutritionally. If you are obese, losing body fat will significantly relieve overall stress on the body. A sensible low-fat diet—as outlined in Chapter 2—will allow you to reduce your body fat level without harming your health or stressing your body.

There are two food supplements that you can take to relieve stress. The first of these is B-complex vitamins, which promote calm and healthy nerves. You can also buy tablets of tryptophan (one of the eight essential amino acids) at health food stores. Tryptophan is an effective natural tranquilizer. By taking two or three tablets of this amino acid, you can induce deep and restful sleep within 30–40 minutes.

The opposite of negative stress is *eustress,* or positive stress. Eustress evokes the same physiological reactions within your body (e.g., increased pulse rate and elevated blood pressure), but it has a very positive effect on the human mind and body. Therefore, you should seek to increase the eustress you experience while simultaneously attempting to decrease the negative stress you experience.

Eustress accompanies all dangerous recreational pursuits, such as mountain climbing, big-game hunting, bullfighting, surfing, and motor racing. Or, eustress can be induced by such emotion-charged events as falling in love or returning home from a long trip.

Eustress is so pleasurable that many men and women literally exist for their next encounter with it. Perhaps you know a woman in your office or a neighbor who loves to sky dive on weekends. Only when she is stepping out of a plane thousands of feet above the ground is she truly happy and fully alive. All during the rest of the week she is morose, almost like a wild animal caged in a zoo, as she awaits the coming weekend and her next adrenalin-laden eustress "fix."

You can also use small negative distresses to spur yourself on to greater accomplishment in life. Usually this involves putting pressure on yourself to succeed by setting up little goals, each progressively higher than the one before it. As long as you keep such goal-oriented pressures small enough so they don't make you feel compulsive about achieving them, they can be very valuable in furthering your career or athletic pursuits. Both my husband Lou and I use this self-induced stressing technique to further improve our personal and professional lives. And I am happy to report to you that it has always worked extremely well for both of us.

Conclusion

I can't emphasize strongly enough that your mind is the master organ and the most powerful organ in your body. Correctly programmed and utilized, your mind can help you work miracles with your health and appearance. Simply give your mind the chance to help you reach for greatness!

4

Exercise and
Body Sculpture

The final leg of the health and fitness tripod is exercise. Just as a tripod cannot stand on one or two legs without toppling, each of these three health and fitness factors must be developed to the maximum and must interact with the other two for a whole (health and fitness) to be achieved.

Exercise can take many forms, but generally speaking it falls into three basic groups: strength training, aerobic conditioning, and flexibility training.

Weight Training and Bodybuilding

When I first started exercising regularly I concentrated my efforts on aerobic and flexibility training, totally ignoring weight training. But soon after I met my husband, Lou Ferrigno (a former Mr. Universe winner), I gained a greater appreciation for this activity. Now I consider weight training a vital part of my overall exercise program, and I look forward to all of my weight workouts.

Weight training is an essential form of exercise for both men and women because it is the best way to build strength. It is also one of the best ways to sculpture your body—adding and subtracting body contours wherever you wish—because of its selectivity and intensity.

While calisthenics, dance, stretching, and aerobic activities can build a small degree of physical strength, only weight training can build a superior type of physical power. Most of the normal activities you do in your life require little strength, but it's a good idea to have a sizable reserve of physical power to call on in life's emergencies.

Reserve strength could actually save your life in an automobile accident, or in a surprise mugging or assault. Hopefully, these and other catastrophies will never befall you, but if they do, you're better off having great physical strength in reserve.

Selectivity is an important advantage of weight training, because exercises can be chosen to stress single parts of the body and even small segments of a body part. If some small part of your body—such as your calves, buttocks, or bustline—is flabby or skinny, you can correct such deficiencies by working with one or two weight training exercises for the weak area. Other forms of exercise don't offer such specific selectivity.

Weight training can be made very intense, because this form of exercise is much heavier than any other in existence. And by taking shorter rests than normal during a workout, you can make weight training a good aerobic conditioner. It's difficult to find a better way to develop strength and aerobic conditioning than weight training.

Weight training becomes bodybuilding when you use it to add size, shape, and contour to a part of your body. And because of the selectivity and great intensity of weight training, bodybuilding is far and away the best way to sculpt your body, adding or subtracting inches literally wherever you like.

Through weight training I was able rather easily to add firm contours to my thighs and calves, while trimming down my arms, hips, and buttocks.

One commonly voiced objection to weight training is that it decreases flexibility and causes a man or woman to become muscle-bound. If this worries you, you'll be happy to hear that, as early as 1952, scientific studies proved conclusively that weight training actually *improves* flexibility. Indeed, my husband—a champion competitive bodybuilder with huge muscles—is far more flexible than an average person. In fact, he's the most flexible person I know, despite his huge body mass!

A second common but unfounded fear is that weight training will make a woman look unfeminine. To answer this charge, I ask you simply to look at the photos of me in this book. I weight train fairly hard three or four times per week. Am I unfeminine? Certainly not!

Actually, it is totally impossible for a woman to look like a man after even a lifetime of superhard weight training. This is because the male hormone *testosterone* must be present in the human body in large quantities for a person to be able to build muscles as large as a male bodybuilder's. And while women do have small levels of

testosterone in their bodies, a woman with a very high level still has only a fourth of the testosterone that a man with a very low level of this hormone has.

Without testosterone, a woman cannot build big muscles, regardless of how hard, long, and heavy she trains each day. Furthermore, the high levels of *estrogen* (the most prominent feminizing hormone) in our bodies further preclude muscle growth. Indeed, some women bodybuilders have even foolishly taken injections of testosterone, which has disastrous side effects for women, and still have not built large muscles, because their estrogen overwhelms the testosterone in their bodies.

All that weight training will do for a woman is allow her to tone and sculpt her body, *without* making it look more masculine. Believe me, you can train as hard as you want with weights, and you will *never* look masculine.

On the following pages is a series of exercises, with both photos and written descriptions that will allow you to perform each movement correctly without additional coaching. After this group of exercises two workouts you can use to improve your body are described. But first you should know some general rules that will make training safe and effective.

1. Warm up for five to 10 minutes with stretching and calisthenics before weight training.
2. Do all of your exercises in the order listed in each workout, doing all of the groupings (**sets**) of repetitions for an exercise before moving on to the next grouping.
3. Weight train on three nonconsecutive days per week, e.g., Mondays, Wednesdays, and Fridays.
4. Restrict body movement during an exercise to the limbs and joints to be moved in that exercise during your workout.
5. Rest for 45–60 seconds between sets.

6. When an exercise becomes easy for you to do, add 2½ to five pounds to your barbell, dumbbells, or machine.
7. While Universal Gym and Nautilus machines are good forms of exercise, they are costly to own and not as accessible as free weights (barbells and dumbbells).
8. Dress in loose-fitting clothing or a leotard and tights while training. You will need complete freedom of movement in all of your limbs while weight training.
9. Be persistent. The human body doesn't change dramatically in a day, or even a week. It takes considerable time to see meaningful physical changes from any form of exercise. This includes weight training.
10. For additional information on weight training and bodybuilding, consult the sources listed in the bibliography at the end of this book. My hustand also has an excellent series of bodybuilding courses, and all of his advice is applicable to women as well as to men. For information on these courses, write to Lou Ferrigno, PO Box 1671, Santa Monica, CA 90406.

Squat—start.
Squat—finish.

Weight Training Exercises

The following pool of basic exercises will be used to make up the exercise routines with weights at the end of this section. Refer to the photos as you read the exercise descriptions, and you should easily be able to learn the movements correctly.

Squat

Emphasis—This excellent movement strongly stresses the frontal thighs, hips, buttocks, and lower back. Squats also place emphasis on the hamstring muscles at the back of the thighs, the abdominals, and the upper back. And Squats are an excellent movement for burning calories and reducing body fat all over your body.

Lunge—start.

Lunge—midpoint.

Lunge—finish.

Starting Position—Hold a loaded barbell behind your neck and balance it across your shoulders by grasping the handles just inside the plates (the flat discs that help make a barbell heavier). Place your feet at shoulder width and point your toes outward at 45-degree angles. Stare straight ahead and tighten your back muscles so your back remains upright throughout the movement. If you find that you have trouble balancing while squatting, elevate your heels by placing them on a two-by-four-inch board or two barbell plates.

The Movement—Keeping your head up and your back straight, bend your knees and slowly sink down into a full Squat. Your knees should travel out over your feet (i.e., outward at 45-degree angles) as you squat up and down. Without bouncing at the bottom of the movement, slowly straighten your legs and return to the starting position. Repeat for the required number of repetitions.

Breathing—Breathe in and out normally as you pause for a second at the top of each repetition. If you must breathe in and out during the movement, breathe in as you descend and out as you rise up from the squatting position.

Lunge

Emphasis—Lunges done freehand or with weights are good for toning hips and buttocks, as well as for firming and shaping the muscles of the frontal thighs.

Starting Position—With a light barbell held behind your neck, adopt the same starting position as for a Squat, except that you will not have your heels on a two-by-four-inch board. As an alternative to holding a barbell behind your neck, you can hold two light dumbbells in your hands.

The Movement—Step forward as far as you can with your right foot, being sure that you put it down on the floor with your toes pointed straight ahead. Then slowly bend your right knee (keeping your left leg as straight as you can) until your right knee is over your right foot and your left knee is near to or touching the floor. Slowly push back up, accelerating the movement near the top so you can push your right foot back into line with the other foot. Reverse the procedure by stepping out with your left foot. Alternate feet until you have done the required number of repetitions for each leg.

Breathing—Breathe in as you sink down on each repetition and out as you return to the starting point.

Leg Extension

Emphasis—Leg Extensions put direct stress on the frontal thigh muscles, isolating them from all the other muscle groups. If you have weak frontal thigh muscles, this movement will attack those muscles very hard. Leg Extensions are also an excellent exercise for rehabilitating injured knees.

Starting Position—Sit at the edge of a leg extension table and hook your insteps under the lower set of rollers. Grasp the sides of the bench or the handles provided to anchor your upper body in position during the movement.

The Movement—Slowly straighten your legs under the resistance provided by the machine. Pause for a count of two at the top of the movement, then lower back to the starting point. Repeat the movement for the required number of repetitions.

Breathing—Breathe in and out normally at any point in the movement.

Leg Curl

Emphasis—This excellent movement directly stresses the hamstring muscles at the back of your thighs. Leg Curls also put secondary emphasis on the calf muscles.

Starting Position—Lie face down on a leg curl bench so that your knees are at the edge of the padded table. Hook your heels

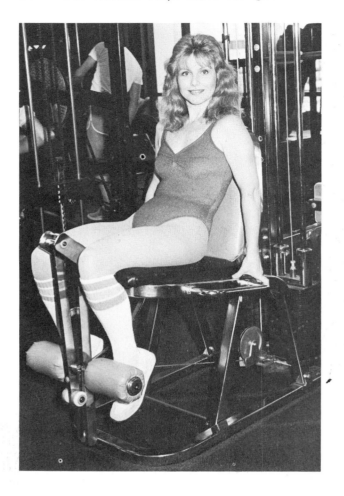

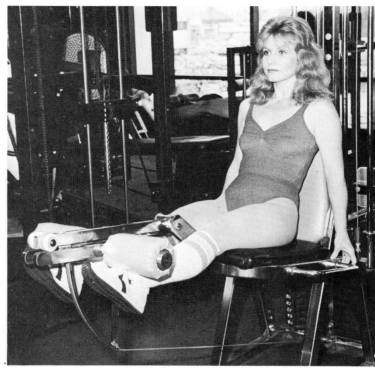

Leg Extension—start.

Leg Extension—finish.

under the upper set of roller pads and grasp either the handles provided or the sides of the bench to steady your body during the movement.

The Movement—Slowly bend your legs fully under the resistance provided by the machine. Hold the top position for a count of one or two, then lower slowly back to the starting point. Repeat the movement for the required number of repetitions.

Breathing—Breathe in and out normally at any point in the movement.

Upright Rowing

Emphasis—This movement is primarily for the trapezius muscles of the upper back, as well as for the deltoids and biceps. Well-toned trapezius muscles help you maintain ideal shoulder posture, so if posture is a

problem for you, be sure to do a few extra sets of Upright Rowing.

Starting Position—Stand erect and grasp the middle of a barbell handle so your index fingers are four to six inches apart and your palms are facing your body. Your arms should be hanging straight down along your sides so the barbell rests across your upper thighs.

The Movement—Slowly pull the barbell straight up to your chin, keeping it close to your body along the entire route from your thighs to your chin. As you pull the weight upward, emphasize getting your elbows up higher than your hands all along the route, but especially at the top of the movement. Lower slowly back to the starting point and repeat the movement for the required number of repetitions.

Breathing—Breathe in as you raise the

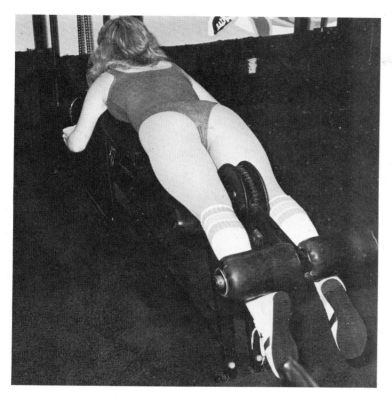

Leg Curl—start.

barbell upward and out as you lower it back down to the starting point.

Good Morning

Emphasis—This exercise is primarily aimed at stressing the lower back muscles, but it also puts emphasis on the hamstring muscles at the back of your thighs. If you suffer from a weak lower back, do a couple of extra sets of Good Mornings each time you train with weights.

Starting Position—Stand erect and balance a barbell behind your neck in the same position you would assume for a set of Squats but with your feet pointed directly ahead. Bend your knees slightly.

The Movement—Keeping your knees bent slightly, bend over forward until your torso is parallel to the floor. Straighten back up to the starting position and repeat the movement for the required number of repetitions.

Breathing—Breathe out as you bend over and in as you return to the starting position.

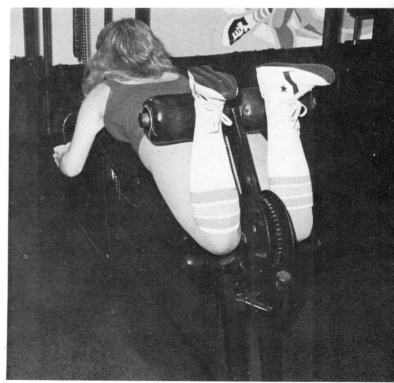

Leg Curl—finish.

Upright Rowing—start.

Upright Rowing—finish.

Good Morning—start.

Good Morning—finish.

Barbell Bent Rowing—start.

Barbell Bent Rowing—finish.

Bench Press—start.

Bench Press—finish.

Barbell Bent Rowing

Emphasis—This is one of my husband's favorite movements for upper back strength and muscularity. I like it myself for both of these reasons, as well as for the toning effect it has on my whole back.

Starting Position—Stand up next to a barbell that is lying on the floor so that your toes are about six inches behind the bar. Bend over at the waist until your torso is parallel to the floor, then bend your knees slightly. Take a shoulder-width grip on the barbell with your palms facing your legs.

The Movement—Maintaining this position, bend your arms and slowly pull the barbell up until its handle touches the lower edge of your rib cage. Return the barbell to the starting position and repeat the movement for the required number of repetitions, not quite touching the floor with the barbell at the bottom point of each repetition. As you pull the barbell up, be sure that your upper arms travel outward at 45-degree angles from your torso.

Breathing—Breathe in as you raise the weight upward and out as you lower it back to the starting position.

Bench Press

Emphasis—This movement works the entire chest area, firming and strengthening the muscles underlying your bust to lift and support it. Bench Presses also stress the shoulder muscles and the triceps at the back of your upper arms.

Starting Position—Lie on your back on a flat exercise bench. Take a shoulder-width grip on a light barbell with your palms facing your feet. Support the barbell at arm's length directly above your chest.

The Movement—Being sure that your elbows travel directly out to the sides, bend your arms and lower the barbell until it touches the middle of your chest. Return to the starting position by straightening your arms. Repeat the movement for the required number of repetitions. Be sure that the barbell travels directly up and down during the movement.

Breathing—Breathe in as you lower the barbell to your chest and out as you push it back up to the starting point.

Incline Flye

Emphasis—This dumbell exercise stresses the upper pectoral muscles, lifting the bustline.

Starting Position—Lie back on a 45-degree incline bench and grasp two light dumbbells in your hands. Push the dumbbells up to arm's length above your chest so that your arms are perpendicular to the floor. Bend your arms slightly at the elbows.

The Movement—Being sure that your arms travel directly out to the sides into a crucifix position, move the dumbbells in semicircles to as low a position out to your sides as possible. Return the dumbbells back along the same arcs to the starting point and repeat the movement for the required number of repetitions.

Breathing—Breathe in as you lower the weights out to the sides and out as you return the dumbbells back to the starting point.

Pec Deck Flye

Emphasis—This movement is good for the chest muscles, because you can work the pectorals without also having to stress the deltoids and/or triceps. This isolation effect can make the Pec Deck Flye a very intense movement for the pectorals.

Starting Position—Raise the seat of the Nautilus double-chest machine as high as it will go. Then sit on the seat and force the inner edges of your forearms against the insides of the vertical pads. Stretch your arms back behind you as far as possible.

Incline Flye—start.

Incline Flye—finish.

Pec Deck Flye—start, left; finish, above.

Military Press—start.

Military Press—finish.

The Movement—From this starting position, tense your pectoral muscles and force the vertical pads toward each other until they touch in front of your torso. Return to the starting point and repeat the movement for the required number of repetitions.

Breathing—Breathe out as you move the pads together and in as you return them to the starting position.

Military Press

Emphasis—This basic exercise works the deltoid muscles of your shoulders as well as the triceps at the back of your upper arms.

Starting Position—Bend over and take a shoulder-width grip on a barbell so your palms are facing your shins. Dip your hips and with leg and back strength pull the barbell up to your shoulders. Stand erect with the barbell at your shoulders and move your elbows directly under the bar.

The Movement—Keeping your elbows under the bar for the entire movement, straighten your arms and push the weight up past your face until your arms are locked and the barbell is directly above your head. Lower back to the starting position and repeat the movement for the required number of repetitions.

Breathing—Exhale as you raise the weight and inhale as you lower it back to the starting point.

Side Lateral

Emphasis—This movement is an isolation exercise for the deltoid muscles of your shoulders.

Starting Position—Stand erect and hold two dumbbells against the fronts of your thighs. Bend your arms slightly at the elbows and maintain this position throughout the movement.

The Movement—Keeping your arms bent slightly, raise the dumbbells directly out to the sides and upward in semicircles until they are above an imaginary line drawn parallel to the floor and through your shoulder joints. Be sure that your palms face downward throughout the movement. Slowly lower back to the starting point and repeat the movement for the required number of repetitions.

Breathing—Breathe in as you lower the weights and out as you raise them.

Side Lateral—start.

Side Lateral—finish.

Barbell Curl—start.

Barbell Curl—finish.

Lying Triceps Extension—start, left; finish, above.

Barbell Curls

Emphasis—This basic movement primarily works the biceps muscles at the front of your upper arms, with secondary emphasis on the forearm muscles.

Starting Position—Stand erect with a barbell in your hands and the bar resting across your upper thighs. You should have a shoulder-width grip on the barbell with your palms facing away from your body. Pin your upper arms to your sides.

The Movement—Keeping your upper arms motionless, use biceps strength to move the barbell in a semicircle from your thighs to your chin. Lower back along the same arc to the starting position and repeat the movement for the required number of repetitions.

Breathing—Breathe in as you curl the weight up and out as you return the barbell to the starting point.

Lying Triceps Extension

Emphasis—This exercise is a favorite of mine for firming and toning the triceps muscles at the back of the upper arms. Flabby upper arms are a common complaint of most women, and this exercise can tighten up that sagging tissue at the back of your upper arms.

Starting Point—Lie back on a flat bench and take a narrow grip (index fingers about six inches apart) in the middle of a barbell. Your palms should face your feet when the barbell is supported at arm's length directly above your chest.

The Movement—Keeping your upper arms in the same position throughout the movement, bend your elbows slowly to lower the barbell in a semicircle to your forehead. Touch your forehead lightly and then return the barbell with triceps strength along the same arc to the starting point. Repeat this movement for the required number of repetitions.

Breathing—Breathe in as you lower the weight to your forehead and out as you push it back to the starting point.

Standing Calf Machine Raise

Emphasis—Rising up and down on your toes on this machine will work the gastrocnemius muscles of your calves very hard, giving them a shape like that of an experienced dancer.

Standing Calf Machine—start.

Standing Calf Machine—finish.

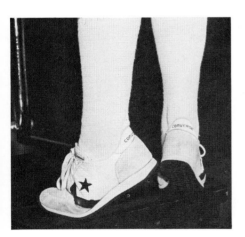

Standing Calf Machine—
finish, toes out.

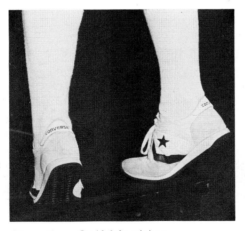

Standing Calf Machine—
finish, toes in.

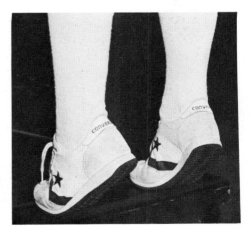

Standing Calf Machine—
finish, toes straight ahead.

Starting Position—Place your shoulders up under the pads on the machine's yoke and put the balls of your feet on the wooden block resting on the floor. Straighten your legs and body and relax your calves to stretch your heels below your toes as far as you can. Your feet should be six to eight inches apart on the block. Your feet should also be placed so they are parallel to each other.

The Movement—From this basic starting position, rise up as high as you can on your toes. Return to the fully stretched starting position and repeat the movement for the required number of repetitions. For variety, you can do raises on a calf machine with your toes pointed outward at a 45-degree angle or inward at a 45-degree angle as well as with your toes pointed directly ahead.

Breathing—Exhale and inhale normally at any part of the movement.

Seated Calf Machine Raise

Emphasis—This is a variation of the Standing Calf Machine Raise that is simply done when seated. It still stresses the gastrocnemius muscles of the calves. But more importantly, it stresses the broad, flat soleus muscles lying under the gastrocnemii. These soleus muscles can be fully contracted only when the knees are bent at a 90-degree angle, as they are in this particular movement.

Starting Position—Sit on the machine's seat, place your toes on the toe crossbar, and force your knees under the knee pads. Then simply push down slightly with your toes and push the stop bar forward to release the machine for your Calf Raises. If you don't have such a machine, simply pad the middle of a barbell with a towel and place it across your knees.

The Movement—Stretch your heels as far below the level of your toes as you can. Then rise up as far as possible on your toes and the balls of your feet. Lower back to the fully stretched position and repeat the movement for the required number of repetitions.

Breathing—As on the Standing Calf Machine Toe Raises, breathe normally in and out at any convenient point in the exercise.

Barbell Calf Raise

Emphasis—This is a free-weight version of Calf Raises using a barbell instead of the standing calf machine. It strongly stresses the gastrocnemius muscles of your lower legs.

Starting Position—Place a barbell behind your neck as in the starting position for a Squat. Place the toes and balls of your feet on a four-by-four-inch block of wood. Be sure that your toes are pointed directly ahead. Then, on successive sets, turn your toes inward and outward.

The Movement—Slowly rise up and down on your toes, being sure to keep your body in balance as you do the movement.

Breathing—As for all calf movements, breathe in and out normally at any convenient point in the exercise.

Leg Raise

Emphasis—This movement stresses the frontal abdominal muscles, with particular emphasis on the lower abdomen. Many women with bulging tummies have discovered that this exercise is the answer to their problems.

Starting Position—Lie on your back on the floor or on an abdominal exercise board. Grasp a heavy piece of furniture or the strap or rollers of the abdominal board behind your head to steady your body for the movement. Slightly bend your legs to take potential stress off your lower back.

The Movement—Keeping your legs bent, raise your feet in semicircles until they are perpendicular to your torso. Lower your legs back to the starting point and repeat the movement for the required number of repetitions.

Breathing—Breathe out as you raise your legs upward and in as you lower them back to the starting point.

Sit-Ups

Emphasis—This commonly used exercise stresses the frontal abdominal muscles, particularly in the upper section.

Seated Calf Machine—start.

Seated Calf Machine —finish.

Starting Position—Lie on your back on an abdominal exercise board and hook your feet under the strap or rollers provided to restrain them. If you don't have an abdominal board, lie on your back on the floor and slide your toes under the edge of a sofa or heavy chair. In both variations, be sure to bend your knees about 10–15 degrees. Doing Sit-Ups with your legs straight is very hard on the lower back. Place your hands behind your neck and interlace your fingers to maintain this position throughout the movement.

The Movement—Slowly curl your shoulders and then your torso off the floor, until you are sitting fully upright. Slowly lower your torso back to the starting point and repeat the movement for the required number of repetitions.

Breathing—Breathe out as you sit up and in as you return back to the starting point.

Knee-Ups

Emphasis—Knee-Ups stress the frontal abdominal muscles, particularly the muscles of the lower abdomen. Like Leg Raises, Knee-Ups are a good exercise for solving the problem of "lower tummy buldge."

Starting Position—Sit at one end of an exercise bench or a chair. Grasp the edges of the bench or chair. Lean backward so your torso is at a 45-degree angle with the floor. Straighten your legs so they make one long line with your torso.

The Movement—Slowly bend your legs and pull your knees up to your chest, keeping your knees fairly close together. Slowly lower your legs back to the starting point and repeat the movement for the required number of repetitions.

Breathing—Breathe out as you pull your knees up and in as you lower your legs back to the starting point.

Barbell Calf Raise—start.

Barbell Calf Raise—finish.

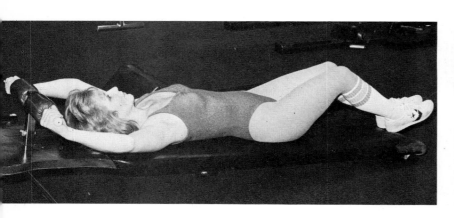

Leg Raise—start.

Leg Raise—finish.

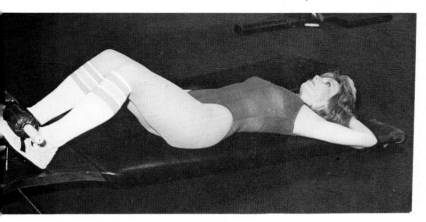

Sit-Up—start.

Sit-Up—finish.

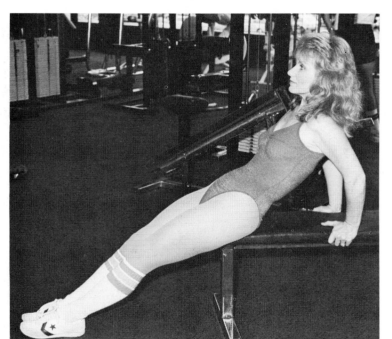

Knee-Up—start.

Knee-Up—finish.

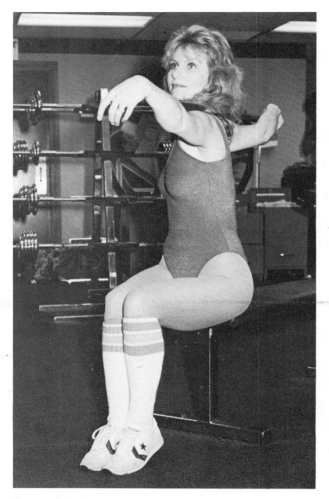

Seated Twisting—start.

Seated Twisting—finish.

Seated Twisting

Emphasis—Seated Twisting firms and tones the muscles at the sides of your waist, causing your waistline to look narrow.

Starting Position—Sit on a flat bench as shown or wrap your ankles around the vertical supports. Your legs and hips should be immobilized during the movement. Place a broomstick or an unloaded barbell bar behind your neck and wrap your arms around it.

The Movement—Twist your shoulders and torso as far as possible to the right. Then immediately and forcefully twist as far as you can to the left. Twist rhythmically from side to side until you have done the required number of repetitions to each side.

Breathing—Simply breathe normally in and out at any point in the movement.

Weight Training Workouts

Most women should spend two or three weeks doing calisthenics conditioning (explained in the next section of this chapter) before commencing a weight training program. This is because weight training is a very intense form of exercise, and your muscles would become extremely sore if you started a weight training program without some preconditioning.

For the first week of your training you should also do only one set of each movement. Then, during the second week, you

CONDITIONING ROUTINE
Monday-Wednesday-Friday

Exercise	Sets	Reps	Starting Weight
Sit-Ups	1-2	15-25	0%
Seated Twisting	1-2	25-50	0%
Leg Extension	3	10-15	25%
Leg Curl	2	10-15	15%
Barbell Bent Rowing	3	8-12	30%
Bench Press	3	8-12	25%
Upright Rowing	2	8-12	20%
Barbell Curl	2	8-12	20%
Lying Triceps Extension	2	8-12	15%
Barbell Calf Raise	3	15-20	30%

can begin to do two sets of each exercise that requires two or three sets. And beginning with the third week, you can do the full workout. This gradual break-in procedure will also help you avoid muscle soreness.

If you *do* become sore, long and hot baths will help relieve the soreness. You will also find that after a second workout your sore muscles will return almost to normal.

Being sure to incorporate all of the weight training tips we've discussed, you can use the general body toning and conditioning workout chart above.

Gaining Weight

To gain firm body weight (refer also to the section on the weight-gain diet in Chapter 2), it is necessary to use heavier weights than would be used when toning, conditioning, and body sculpting. In the following routine, most of the exercises require two or three sets. Do the first set with a moderate weight for 12 repetitions (or 10 reps if only two sets are done). Add 5-10 pounds to the bar or machine and do 10 reps for your second set (or eight if only two sets are

WEIGHT GAIN ROUTINE
Monday-Wednesday-Friday

Exercise	Sets	Reps
Leg Raise	2-3	20-30
Knee-Ups	2-3	20-30
Squat	3	12-8
Leg Curl	2	10-8
Barbell Bent Rowing	3	12-8
Upright Rowing	2	10-8
Good Morning	2	12-10
Bench Press	3	12-8
Incline Flye	2	10-8
Side Lateral Raise	2	10-8
Barbell Curl	2	10-8
Lying Triceps Extension	2	10-8
Seated Calf Machine Raise	2-3	15-10
Standing Calf Machine Raise	2-3	15-10

done). And on the third set, if you do one, and 5–10 more pounds and perform eight reps.

Follow the preceding suggestions and try the workout on the bottom of page 49 if you want to gain weight. (Since this is an advanced routine, you won't need suggested starting weights; once you have reached the advanced level, you'll know what to use from the poundages you are already using.)

Weight training can dramatically improve your athletic ability. Because your muscles will become much stronger with weight training, you will be able to hit a golf ball farther, wallop a tennis ball with greater authority, and participate better in any. other sports activity you prefer.

Calisthenics and Aerobic Classes

Calisthenics have always been popular with fitness-minded women. And in recent years these exercises have been done to music in very popular aerobic exercise/aerobic dance programs. Both of these forms of exercise are excellent, though they are not as intense as weight training.

On the following pages are a number of calisthenic exercises that I use at least three times per week in my physical conditioning and body shaping program. Combined with weight training, stretching, and aerobic activity, such calisthenic workouts have given me a high level of physical fitness.

Knee Push-Ups

To firm and tone your chest, shoulder, and arm muscles, lie face down on the floor, bend your knees to elevate your feet out of the movement, and place your palms on the floor on each side of your chest with your fingers facing forward. Stiffen your torso into a straight position and push your shoulders up off the floor by straightening your arms. Lower your torso back to the

floor and repeat the movement for the required number of repetitions.

Rear Leg Lifts

To firm your buttocks, kneel on the floor and lean forward to place your hands on the floor in the same position you would take to crawl. Extend your left leg backward and straighten it so that your toes on the left foot just touch the floor. Keeping your leg straight, raise it directly upward as high as you can. Lower and raise it again until you have completed the required number of repetitions. Be sure to do an equal number of sets and reps for your right leg.

Side Leg Raises

To tone your hips, lie on the floor on your left side, supporting your torso on your left arm and elbow. Starting with your legs straight and pressed together, raise your right leg upward as high as possible. Lower and repeat for the required number of repetitions. Be sure to do an equal number of sets and repetitions for your left leg.

Scissor Leg Raises

To tone your hips and inner thighs, assume the same starting position as for Side Leg Raises. Raise your upper leg until it is at a 45-degree angle from the floor. Leaving that leg in this position throughout the exercise, raise your lower leg directly upward until it touches the upper leg. Lower slowly and repeat the movement for the required number of repetitions. Be sure to do an equal number of sets and reps for both sides of your body.

Standing Leg Swing

To tone your hips and upper thighs, stand with your right side next to a high stool or countertop and grasp that object with your

Knee Push-Up—
start.

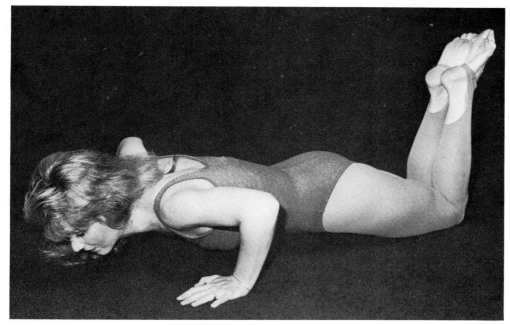

Knee Push-Up—
finish.

right hand to support your torso during the movement. Anchor your right foot in place, stiffen your left leg with a slight bend in it, and then swing your left leg as high up directly to the back and then to the front as you can. Your leg should swing freely, somewhat like the pendulum in a grandfather clock. Be sure to do an equal number of sets and repetitions for your right leg.

Kneeling Jazz Kicks

To firm your buttocks, lower back, and the back of your thighs, assume the same starting position as for Rear Leg Lifts. Bend your left leg fully and tuck it in against your rib cage. Lower your chin to your chest. Then simultaneously arch your back and throw your head backward, while extending

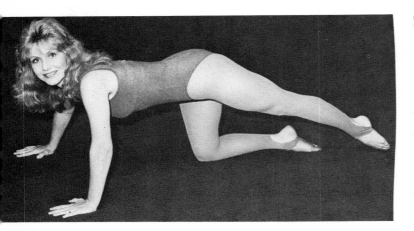

Rear Leg Lift—start.

Rear Leg Lift—finish.

Side Leg Raise—start.

Side Leg Raise—finish.

Scissor Leg Raise—start.

Scissor Leg Raise—finish.

Standing Leg Swing—start.

Standing Leg Swing—finish.

Kneeling Jazz Kick—start.

Kneeling Jazz Kick—finish.

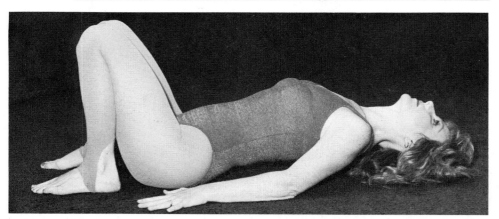

Pelvic Tuck—start.

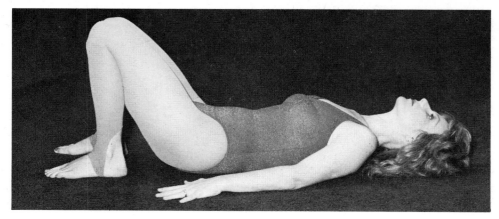

Pelvic Tuck—finish.

Side Stretch—start.

Alternate Toe Stretch—start.

Alternate Toe Stretch—midpoint one, below left; midpoint two, below right.

Lunge—start.

Lunge—finish.

your left leg straight and as high to the back as possible. Repeat for the required number of repetitions. Be sure to do an equal number of sets and repetitions for your right leg.

Pelvic Tuck

To firm and tone your lower back and buttocks, lie on your back on the floor. Place your palms flat on the floor beside your hips and bend your legs until you can place your feet flat on the floor with your heels as close to your buttocks as possible. From this position, slowly flatten your spine on the floor and then squeeze your buttocks together for a count of six. Slowly relax your buttocks and then repeat this flexing movement for the required number of repetitions.

Alternate Toe Touch

To tone your entire midsection, and particularly the sides of your waist and your lower back, stand erect with your feet spread 2–2½ feet apart. Extend your arms out to the sides. Then bend and twist toward the left and touch your right hand to your left foot. Return to the start and repeat the movement toward the right foot. Alternate from side to side for the required number of repetitions.

Lunges

To fully tone and firm your thighs, buttocks, and hips, begin by standing erect with your heels 8–10 inches apart and your hands on your hips. (As you get used to the movement, you can hold your heels together as shown in the photo.) Step forward as far as you comfortably can with your left foot.

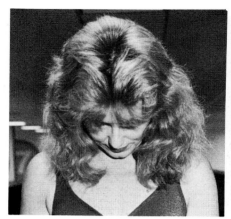

Neck Roll—second position.

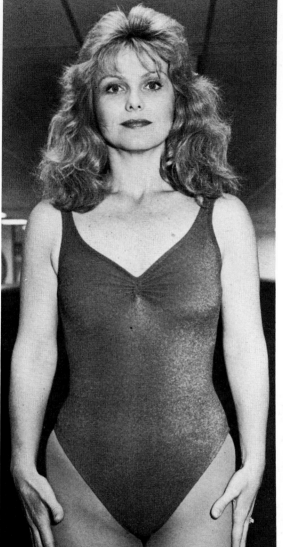

Neck Roll—third position.

Neck Roll—fifth position.

Neck Roll—start.

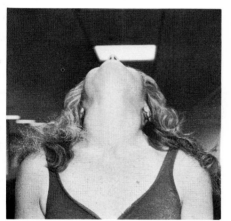

Neck Roll—fourth position.

Keeping your right leg as straight as possible, bend your left leg fully. Push back to the starting point and repeat with your right leg stepping forward. Alternate legs for the required number of repetitions.

Neck Rolls

To firm your neck and jawline, and to relieve neck and upper back tension, start by standing erect with your feet set a comfortable distance apart and your arms down at your sides. Begin the actual movement by dropping your chin to your chest. Roll your head to the left side, then to the back, then to the right, and finally back to the front. After rolling your head several times in this direction, repeat, rolling your head several times in the opposite direction.

Depending on your initial fitness level, you can do these 10 exercises one after the other for 10–60 minutes. Simply do enough repetitions of each movement to feel fatigue developing in the working muscles. Then move on to the next exercise, rotating from one to the next for as long as you feel you need to continue exercising.

Aerobic classes are merely an extension of these calisthenic movements. The exercises are done to music by groups of women with an instructor or leader. Such classes usually last for 60–90 minutes, and they can provide both a good workout and a lot of enjoyment.

Most dance studios offer aerobic exercise/aerobic dance classes. Look in the Yellow Pages of your telephone directory for studios near where you live and take trial lessons at several of them. Then pick the one you like the most and that fits into your schedule and stick with it.

Dance Classes

There are numerous types of dance classes that you can take, and all of them are excellent and enjoyable physical activities. If you want to get into good physical condition and enjoy doing it, take two or three ballet, disco, modern dance, or other dance classes each week.

Dance classes are valuable to any fitness- and health-minded woman, because they develop an unequaled combination of strength, aerobic fitness, and flexibility. And dance also helps you develop unparalleled grace of movement while you are getting into top physical condition.

Aerobic Activities

All forms of aerobic activity develop endurance like no other type of exercise. And the long-lasting, low-intensity activity is very good for heart, vascular, and pulmonary health. In fact, many physical fitness authorities have linked daily aerobic training with greater longevity. Being able to complete a marathon run (a distance of 26 miles, 385 yards), for example, is said to make a man or woman heart attack-proof for life. And finally, aerobic activity tends to increase daily overall energy levels.

Running

Running is the most popular form of aerobics at the present time. An estimated 11 percent of American men and women of all ages run regularly. As I mentioned earlier, my husband and I often participate in this aerobic activity together.

Running and walking are among the easiest aerobic activities to learn, and they are the least expensive to take up. Every man and woman with full use of his or her body was an excellent runner as a child, so all that is necessary to learn to run again is to do it for a few days. You will find that it comes back to you quite naturally.

All one requires to take up running is a $25–$50 pair of jogging shoes (available in any athletic equipment or running equipment store) and the great outdoors, be it rural or urban. Some people, including Lou and myself, like to run on tracks at times, but this is not necessary if you don't have one available.

If you are heavy-busted, it would be a good idea to wear a support bra when you run. These are available at all running stores, as well as at many clothing shops.

The best way to begin a running program is to walk daily for two weeks, working up to from 10–15 minutes the first day to at least 30 minutes per day for the entire second week. This will precondition your legs and cardiorespiratory system enough so you can jog easily and continually for 10–15 minutes, 3–4 days per week when you actually start running. With time, you'll be able to run faster and faster, as well as for up to an hour or more 4–7 days per week. By the time you reach this point (in six months to a year), you will be very, very fit aerobically.

While you will very quickly learn how to

run again, there are 10 safety rules that you should follow when engaged in a running program.

1. **Wear good-quality running shoes.** This is particularly vital if you run on hard surfaces like concrete. These shoes are engineered to absorb the shock of each foot plant while running, and such shock absorption protects the feet, ankles, shins, knees, hips, and back from running-related injuries. Cheap sneakers simply don't protect the feet thoroughly enough.

2. **Always combine running with stretching and weight training.** Running by itself develops only endurance, not all-around physical fitness. You will need to stretch to develop flexibility and lift weights or do some other type of exercises to develop strength if you want to achieve optimum physical fitness.

3. **Never run more than two days in a row.** Most running injuries occur because an athlete runs every day and doesn't allow her body time to rest and recuperate. By allowing one day of rest for every day or two of running, you prevent minor joint and muscle injuries from maturing into painful major injuries.

4. **Run within your capabilities.** The harder you exert yourself while running, the more likely it is that you will suffer an injury. Run easily and in a relaxed, playful manner. It's far better to run easily for a set period of time than it is to use a stopwatch and time yourself repeatedly over a set distance.

5. **Avoid racing.** This is an extension of rule number four above. Racing always leads to running hard, which greatly augments the chance of incurring a serious injury.

6. **Don't run on an uneven surface.** Enough stresses and strains are placed on the feet and legs just from running on a flat surface. Running on a slanted roadside or across a rutted field or lawn greatly magnifies the risk of injury.

7. **Don't try "running through an injury."** Pain is nature's signal that something is injured. Nine times out of ten, continuing to run when you are injured will make a minor injury much worse. Rest is the best way to heal an injury incurred while running, so take 3–5 days off from running whenever you sense that you have injured yourself.

8. **Progress slowly.** You can put excessive stress on your feet and legs by building up your training mileage too rapidly. Do not increase your weekly

mileage total by more than 5% from one week to the next.

9. **Dress warmly in cold weather.** And, conversely, wear a minimum amount of clothing (and a hat) when it is very hot. In cold weather, two or three thin layers of clothing will be warmer than one thick layer.

10. **Make running an enjoyable habit.** To make progress, you must run regularly. But in order to run regularly, you must enjoy it. An unenjoyable type of exercise will quickly be abandoned.

To achieve positive results from running, you must push your pulse rate over 120 beats per minute for at least 12 minutes. I don't believe, however, that any woman needs to run for more than 30–45 total minutes.

If you've been physically inactive, begin your running program by walking. I can't stress this point enough! Then, after two or three weeks of regular walking, you can begin to intersperse periods of two or three minutes of running with two or three minutes of walking. Gradually you will be able to run more and walk less, until you are up to a full, easy 15 consecutive minutes of jogging.

Here is a typical 10-week program of more and more intense running that you can use as a model for building up your own training mileage (quantities are listed in minutes of running).

Week	Day 1	Day 2	Day 3	Total
1	15	15	15	45
2	17	15	15	47
3	17	16	16	49
4	17	17	17	51
5	18	18	17	53
6	19	18	18	55
7	19	19	19	57
8	20	20	19	59
9	20	21	20	61
10	21	21	21	63

Swimming

Swimming is in some ways superior to running as an aerobic exercise activity, though it is more difficult to find a place to swim than it is to locate one where you can run. Some pools also charge a substantial fee, which you needn't worry about when running.

Essentially, swimming offers a superior way to achieve outstanding aerobic conditioning for the whole body but without the injury potential of running. With every running step the body's entire jarring weight is supported on one foot, one ankle, one knee, and one hip, which can, and often does, lead to stress-related leg injuries. On the other hand, when you swim, the water supports most of the weight of your body, greatly lessening stress on your joints.

Bicycling

Bicycling has grown rapidly in popularity in recent years. It offers a superior means of achieving aerobic fitness, while also minimizing strain on the body's joints. Since the bicycle's seat supports your body weight, there is very little strain on the feet, ankles, and knees.

The only real drawback to bicycling is the potential for injury when either falling off a bike or being hit by a careless motorist. Such accidents are rare, of course, but when they do occur the potential for injury is high. In all, however, bicycling is one of my favorite forms of aerobic exercise, because I enjoy the freedom of cruising along out of doors, viewing all of nature's beauties at my leisure.

Aerobic Programs for Fat Loss

Aerobic exercise is excellent for weight loss. Depending on how hard you work at it (i.e., how fast you go), you can burn off 250–700 calories per hour of aerobic activ-

ity. The following chart shows how many calories you can typically burn off through one hour of continuous exercise in each of several forms of aerobic conditioning:

Activity	Calories
Running (10 mph)	900
Bicycling (15 mph)	700
Swimming (1 mph)	650
Racquetball	500
Tennis	400
Basketball	300
Walking (3 mph)	200

Recent research has shown that aerobic activity actually burns more fat than higher-intensity, shorter-duration anaerobic activities such as fast running and fast swimming. This is because aerobic activity tends to increase the body's basal metabolic rate (BMR), causing you to continue burning off body fat at a faster rate long after you've stopped exercising.

The key to using aerobic exercise to lose body fat is *regularity*. Working out three days in a row and then getting lazy and doing nothing for 10 days will have very little effect. Instead, you'd be better off running or bicycling every other day, but regularly. And you'd get the best results from 15–30 minutes of various types of aerobic activity *every day*.

Yoga and Stretching

The final key element of physical fitness is flexibility, which you can achieve best through practicing yoga or regularly performing a series of stretching exercises. Adding flexibility to strength and endurance allows you to perform optimally in all physical activities.

Yoga is one of the easiest and most enjoyable ways to achieve flexibility. The slow, gently stretched yoga *asanas* (postures) can often give you optimum flexibility more rapidly than faster, more forceful stretching. This is due to the action of your body's "stretch reflex," a protective mechanism that keeps you from inadvertently stretching a muscle too far and tearing it.

To illustrate how the stretch reflex works, imagine yourself running at night and not seeing a four-inch-high stone in your path. If the toes of one foot came down forcefully on the stone and you didn't have a stretch reflex, you could stretch your heel so far below the level of your toes that the stretch would tear your calf muscle.

At the first hint of this type of quick stretch, however, your stretch reflex mechanism senses the impending trauma and contracts the calf muscle before it can be stretched too far. This contraction has a shock absorber effect, as it shortens the muscle progressively to prevent a tear.

If you are doing a stretching exercise and bouncing too quickly into the stretch, your stretch reflex mechanism shortens the working muscles enough so they can't be stretched fully. Thus, when a stretch is done too quickly and forcefully, the muscle can't be stretched fully, and you lose much of the benefit of doing the stretching exercise.

Yoga stretches are slow and gentle and therefore prevent the stretch reflex syndrome. As in yoga asanas, you will achieve a much greater stretch if you stretch slowly than if you simply stretched ballistically.

Yoga classes are available nearly everywhere—through YMCAs and YWCAs, city recreation departments, high schools and colleges, adult education programs, and private studios. As with aerobic dance classes, you should try out several different yoga classes and pick the one that best suits your time schedule and unique personality.

I use a program of stretching exercises to achieve full joint and muscle flexibility. And I am careful to do all of my stretches slowly to avoid activating my stretch reflex. I've found it difficult to achieve results from a stretching routine if I don't do at least a little bit of stretching almost every day.

Here are my favorite stretching exercises.

Hamstring Stretch

To stretch the hamstring muscles at the back of your thighs, sit on the floor with your legs pressed together and held straight out in front of you. Bend forward and grasp your lower legs. (Eventually you should be able to grasp your feet as shown in the photo.) Then use your hands to pull your torso gently forward. Ideally, you will be able to touch your forehead to your knees at the fully stretched point. Hold the full stretch for 10–15 seconds and then relax.

V-Sitting Stretch

To stretch your hamstrings, back muscles, and inner thigh muscles, sit on the floor with your legs spread as wide as possible. Reach to the right and pull your torso down to that leg. Hold the stretch for 10–15 seconds, relax, then stretch for 10–15 seconds to the left. Finally, lean forward between your legs as far as you can, holding that stretch for another 10–15 seconds.

Seated Groin Stretch

To stretch the muscles on the inside of your thighs, sit on the floor and bend your legs fully enough so you can place the soles of your feet together. Then pull your feet inward as far as possible. Finally, push gently outward with your hands on your knees until you reach a fully stretched position. Hold this position for 10–15 seconds and then relax.

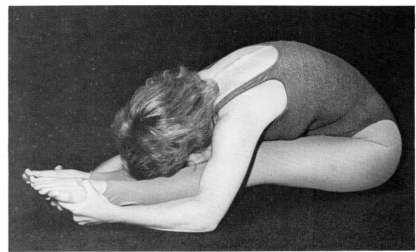

Hamstring Stretch—start, left; finish, below.

Hurdler's Stretch

To stretch the hamstrings, back, and every muscle around your hip girdle, sit on the floor with one leg stretched out ahead of your body and the other bent and placed directly to the rear. In this position, bend as far as possible to the front for 10–15 seconds. Do an equal amount of stretching for the other leg. And, if you are flexible enough to do a full split, go ahead and perform this advanced version.

Torso Stretch

To stretch all of the muscles along the front of your body, particularly those of your abdomen, support yourself on the floor face down on your hands and toes. Your body should be held straight, and your arms and legs should be perfectly straight throughout the movement. Lower your hips to the floor, throw back your head, and

arch your back as much as you can. Hold this position for 10–15 seconds.

Thigh Stretch

To stretch the frontal thigh and hip muscles, stand erect and grasp some object with your right hand to balance your body during the movement. Then bend your left leg fully, reach back with your left hand, and grasp your left ankle. Finally, pull upward on your ankle as high as you comfortably can and hold that stretch for 10–15 seconds. Repeat the stretch for your right leg.

Calf Stretch

To stretch your calf muscles, stand facing a wall. Place your hands on the wall a little below shoulder height and walk your feet backward until your body is leaning into the wall at a 45-degree angle. Keep your legs

V-Sitting Stretch—start.

V-Sitting Stretch—position one.

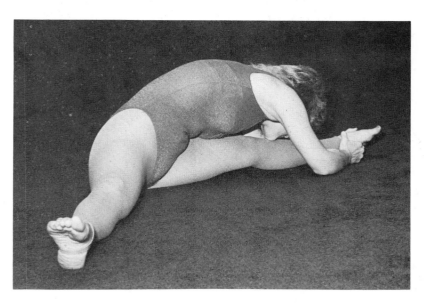

V-Sitting Stretch—position two.

Seated Groin Stretch—start.   Seated Groin Stretch—finish.

Hurdler's Stretch—start.

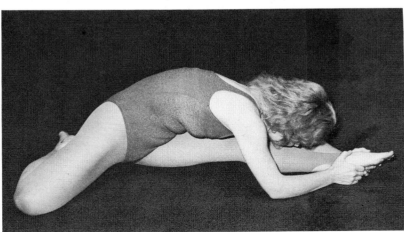

Hurdler's Stretch—finish.

Torso Stretch—start.

Torso Stretch—finish.

Thigh Stretch—start.

Thigh Stretch—finish.

and torso straight throughout the movement. Then simply force your heels down as close to the floor as you can. If you can comfortably hold your heels on the floor for 10–15 seconds, walk out another half-step for your calf stretches in the next workout.

Side Stretch

To stretch all of the muscles along your sides, stand erect with your feet at least shoulder width apart, your hands clasped directly overhead, and your arms straight. Keeping your legs straight, bend as far as you can directly to the left. Hold that stretched position for 10–15 seconds and repeat to the right side.

Chest Stretches

To stretch the muscles of your chest and shoulders, stand with your back toward a high table or countertop. With your arms straight, reach to the rear and place your palms downward on the table or countertop. Keeping your arms straight, slowly bend your legs until you feel a stretching sensation across your chest. Hold this position for 10–15 seconds, relax, and repeat the movement.

Shoulder Stretches

To limber up your shoulders, extend your left arm directly toward the ceiling, then

Side Stretch—start.

Side Stretch—finish.

Chest Stretch—start.

Chest Stretch—finish.

bend your arm fully, extending your left hand down your upper back. Bend your right arm and run your right hand up your back from below. Try to join your hands behind your back in this position. Pull your hands together as far as you comfortably can. Hold this stretched position for 10–15 seconds. Be sure to do an equal amount of stretching on both sides of your body.

Towel Stretch

To stretch your shoulder joints and the muscles of your chest, back, and arms, stand erect with your feet a comfortable distance apart. Grasp a towel with your hands spread a little wider than shoulder width. Your palms should be pointed for-

ward. Then slowly move your hands in a semicircle from your thighs to the small of your back, "dislocating" your shoulders halfway through the movement. Dislocate again on the way back up to the starting position. Repeat the movement several times. The narrower you set your hands on the towel, the more difficult this stretching exercise will be.

A Stretching Program

Do each of these 11 stretching exercises at least once on a daily basis, gradually working up to 40–60 seconds in each stretch. When you have time, you can go through the series up to five or six times, making each stretch a little deeper with every trip

Shoulder Stretch—start, left; finish, right.

Towel Stretch—start, left; midpoint, below left; finish, below right.

through the circuit. This way you can work into a much deeper stretch than you could accomplish without injury when not warmed up.

As with weight training, it's necessary to break into a stretching program gradually. Unless your body is very used to stretching, you can make your muscles excruciatingly sore by trying to do more than one or two easy trips through this 11-exercise stretching circuit.

Optimum Fitness

Optimum physical fitness can be attained by combining weight training and/or calisthenics with an aerobic activity (or two) and a stretching program. And the best way to do this is to make your exercise sessions a daily habit for the rest of your life.

Do a little stretching every day and perhaps some calisthenics on an almost daily basis. You can alternate days of weight training with days of aerobic exercise quite conveniently. Ideally, you should use your stretching as a warm-up for your weight training and aerobic workouts.

Of course, if you're really serious about being in top physical condition, you can combine all three major types of exercise every day. But since it would be difficult to do all of this in a brief daily workout, you should do two or three separate training sessions during the day. As an example, you could run in the morning after you awaken, stretch on your lunch break, and then weight train in the late afternoon or evening.

Conclusion

This has been an exceptionally long chapter because of the variety of exercises you can and should do. Nonetheless, it is an extremely important chapter, because exercise combines sublimely with good nutrition and a positive mental attitude to give you an optimum lifestyle!

5

Couple and Family Fitness

Physical fitness training need not be a solitary, individual pursuit. It can and *should* be an activity that you can share with the man in your life, as well as with every member of your family. Indeed, fitness for couples and families is currently booming in popularity.

Obviously, I could never keep up with Lou in his bodybuilding workouts. He weighs more than twice as much as I do, and he's 10 times as strong. But when he goes to Gold's Gym in Venice, California, to train, I often go with him to do my own weight training, calisthenics, and stretching workouts. And it's much easier and more enjoyable to do my own fitness sessions when I can look across the gym and see Lou training, too.

Outside of the gym, there are innumerable physical activities that we can share. We can do various stretching and calisthenics exercises together, and we can easily perform our aerobic workouts together. We often run, bicycle, or roller-skate along together, and sometimes I bicycle or skate with Lou when he runs at a little faster pace around our neighborhood.

Regardless of what Lou and I do together in our physical fitness sessions, it is valuable to us as a couple, because we are sharing and together when we train. And this principle of togetherness can easily be extended to include the entire family in the health and fitness way of life.

Couple Exercises

With an innovative mind—or, better yet, two of them—you can easily develop a host of exercises to do with the man in your life and/or with your children. On the following pages many of these exercises are described and illustrated.

Partner Sit-Ups/Hyperextensions

With a partner to hold down your feet, it is easy to do both Sit-Ups and Hyperextensions at home, with nothing more than the floor and a high table for equipment. All your partner needs to do is restrain your feet, as in these exercise photos!

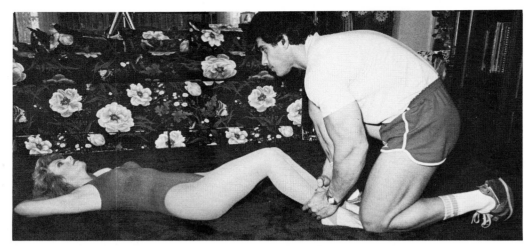

Partner Sit-Up—
start.

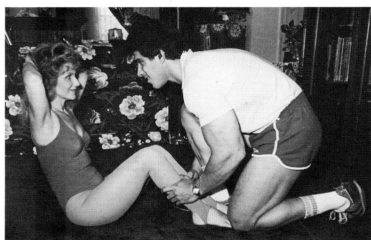

Partner Sit-Up—
finish.

Partner Hyperextension—start.

Partner Hyperextension—finish.

Partner Rowing

Sit down on the floor facing each other and place your feet against your partner's. Bend your knees slightly. Each of you should then grasp a towel with both hands so that about 12 inches of towel shows between your grips. From this basic starting position, pull your hands in to touch your upper abdomen, while your partner extends his arms slowly to give you resistance. Then it's your partner's turn to pull his hands to the upper abdomen while you are resisting the movement. Row back and forth like this for 8–12 repetitions.

Partner Back Stretch

This movement is similar to the foregoing exercise. Adopt the same starting position by sitting on the floor and placing the soles of your feet against those of your partner. Both of you should bend your legs slightly. With palms facing the floor, both of you grasp a broomstick in between you. One of you will have your hands touching each other in the middle of the stick, while the other should place his or her hands on the stick just outside those of the first partner. Alternatively, you can also grip a towel. From this basic starting position, lean backward and pull your partner toward you. Your partner should keep his or her arms straight with the head between the arms to stretch all of the back muscles fully. After holding this position for a few seconds, have your partner pull backward on the stick to help you stretch your own back muscles.

Partner Squat

Sit back to back on the floor, with your feet placed flat on the floor at about shoulder width and approximately 8–10 inches in front of the buttocks. With arms held straight, intertwine your fingers of each hand with those of your partner. From this basic starting position, lean back against your partner and straighten your legs in unison until you are both standing erect. Lower back down to the starting point and repeat the movement for 10–15 repetitions.

Partner Hamstring Stretch

Sit on the floor with your legs extended straight along the floor in front of you. Press your legs together. Lean forward and try to place your torso along the tops of your thighs. Have your partner gently push down on your upper back to help you stretch your hamstring and lower back muscles more intensely.

Donkey Calf Raise

To tone and build up your calf muscles, bend forward at the waist and place your hands on a chair or flat exercise bench to steady your body, with your torso parallel to the floor. Keep your legs straight throughout the movement. For resistance, your partner can push down with his or her hands on your lower back. For him to experience similar resistance, you can sit astride his hips. From the basic starting position, simply rise and then lower yourself back down on your toes for 15–20 repetitions. As with all weight-training calf movements, you can stand with your toes on a block of wood to get a longer range of movement for your Donkey Calf Raises. You can also experiment with angling your toes inward at 45 degrees on some sets, straight ahead on others, and outward at 45 degrees on still other sets of the movement.

Partner Push-Up

While this movement will probably be most beneficial for your stronger male partner, you can also build up and tone your chest, shoulders, and arms with it. Have your partner assume the starting position for a Push-Up and then sit on his shoulders as illustrated. With the resistance

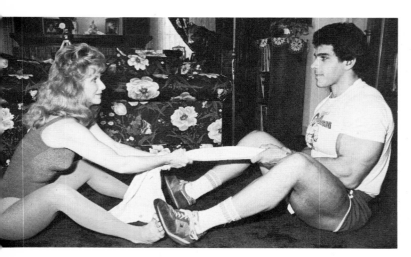

Towel Lat Pull—start.

Towel Lat Pull—finish.

Partner Squat—start.

Partner Squat—finish.

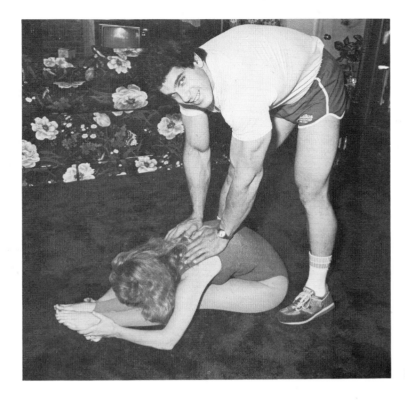

Partner Hamstring Stretch.

Donkey Calf Raise—start.

Donkey Calf Raise—finish.

you provide with your body in this manner, he can do his Push-Ups under great stress. When you do your own Partner Push-Ups, your partner can either push down on your shoulders or pull up on them, according to whether you need resistance or assistance on the movement.

Partner Lateral Raise

You can use this exercise to firm and strengthen your shoulder muscles. Stand facing your partner. Your feet should be placed at about shoulder width and your toes should be about six inches away from his. Close your hands into fists and place your knuckles together about six inches in front of your hips, with the heels of your hands facing each other. Unlock your arms so they are bent about 10–15 degrees and keep them bent at this angle throughout the movement. With his palms facing inward, have your partner grasp your wrists. From this starting position, raise your hands in quarter-circles out to the sides until they are slightly above shoulder height. As you raise your hands like this, your partner should push downward on them just hard enough so you can raise them completely and with some degree of effort in four or five seconds. Then, as you lower your hands back to the starting point, he should push downward even harder while you resist the lowering motion as strongly as possible.

Partner Leg Extension

This movement strengthens and shapes up the quadriceps muscles on the front of your thighs. Sit on a high strong table, a piano bench, or a chair so the backs of your knees are against the edge of the table or seat. Hang your shins directly downward so they are perpendicular to the floor. Your knees and ankles can be held together or about eight inches apart throughout the movement. Once you are in this position,

grasp the edges of the table, bench, or chair to steady your body during the movement. Next, have your partner sit or kneel about two feet in front of you, grasping your ankles. From this basic starting position, slowly straighten your legs as your partner presses against your ankles to provide resistance to your working thigh muscles. He can push even harder as you resist returning your feet and ankles to the starting position.

Partner Leg Curl

You can use Leg Curls to firm and strengthen the hamstring muscles at the back of your thighs. Consistent use of this movement can help you eliminate cellulite on the back of your thighs. Lie face down on the floor, preferably on one that is thickly carpeted. If such a carpet is not available, fold a large bath towel several times and place it under your knees as a pad. Your knees and ankles can be held together or up to eight inches apart throughout the movement. Your partner should kneel on one knee just behind your feet and grasp your ankles with his hands. From this basic starting position, fully bend your legs as your partner provides resistance by pulling back against your ankles. Then he can pull even harder as you strongly resist returning your legs to the beginning straight position.

Partner Triceps Extension

Using just a partner and a hand towel, you can quickly firm up the backs of your upper arms. Stand erect and grasp the towel tightly with both hands. Extend your arms directly overhead so that your upper arms press against the sides of your head throughout the movement. The towel should hang down your back. Your partner can stand facing your back and about a foot away from you. Standing in this position, he should grasp the lower end of the towel

Partner Push-Up—start, below; finish, right.

Partner Lateral Raise—start, left; finish, above.

Partner Leg Extension—
start.

Partner Leg Extension—
finish.

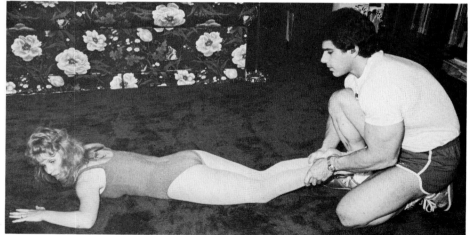

Partner Leg Curl—start.

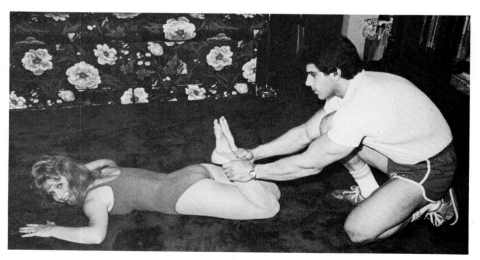

Partner Leg Curl—finish.

with both hands. Bending your elbows and moving *only* your forearms, have your partner pull downward on the towel, while you strongly resist the movement, until your arms are fully bent and your hands are two or three inches behind your neck. Then have your partner lessen his downward pressure on the towel as you slowly straighten your arms.

Partner Shoulder Stretches

To stretch and make more supple your shoulder joints, shoulder muscles, chest muscles, and upper back muscles, stand erect with your arms straight and extended to the rear. Keeping your arms straight throughout the stretch, have your partner pull gently upward on your wrists as far as you can comfortably stretch. Relax and then repeat the movement.

Partner Leg Abduction

This movement is difficult to duplicate in weight training, and yet it is the best one for firming and strengthening the muscles on the sides of your hips and the outsides of your thighs. Lie on your back and place your arms on the floor along the sides of your torso. Lock your knees and keep your legs straight throughout the movement. Have your partner kneel six inches away from your feet. He should then grasp your ankles with his palms facing inward and raise your feet three or four inches from the floor. From this basic starting position, you force your legs as wide apart as possible while your partner resists the movement by pushing your ankles inward. Once you have fully pushed your legs apart, your partner can increase his hand pressure as you resist the closing of your legs.

Partner Leg Adduction

This is the exact opposite of the foregoing movement, and it's a superb exercise for firming up those hard-to-reach muscles on your inner thighs. Both you and your partner should assume the same starting position as for Partner Leg Abductions, except that your partner should grasp your ankles with his palms facing outward rather than inward. In this movement he should push outward against your ankles, forcing your legs completely apart as you resist this movement. Then he can lessen his outward pressure as you force your legs back together. As with Partner Leg Abductions, you should keep your legs straight throughout the exercise.

Partner Arm Curls

This movement will firm the biceps muscles on the front of your upper arms. Stand erect, facing your partner, with your toes about one foot from his. Extend your arms down at your sides with your palms facing forward. Your partner should close his hands into fists and place them in your hands with the knuckles facing downward. Grasp your partner's fists and pin your upper arms against the sides of your torso. Keep them in this position throughout the movement. Bending your elbows and moving only your forearms, slowly move your hands in semicircles from the tops of your thighs to your chin. As you execute this movement, your partner should press against your hands with his fists to provide resistance against your working biceps. At the top of the movement, he can increase his pressure to slowly force your hands back to the starting position.

These are just a few of the many partner resistance exercises that you can develop. Just use a little imagination in making up others!

When you do these partner resistance movements with a man as strong as my husband Lou, it will be impossible for you

Partner Triceps Extension—start.

Partner Triceps Extension—finish.

Partner Shoulder Stretch—start.

Partner Shoulder Stretch—finish.

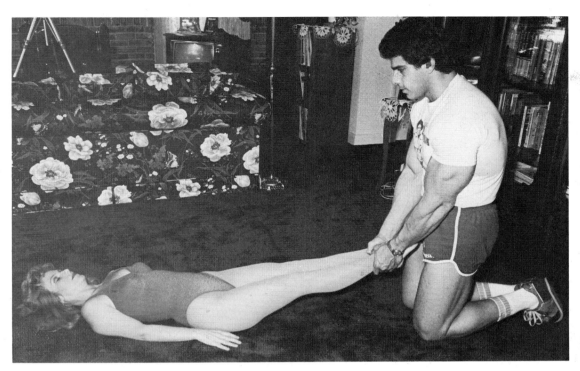

Partner Leg Abduction—start.

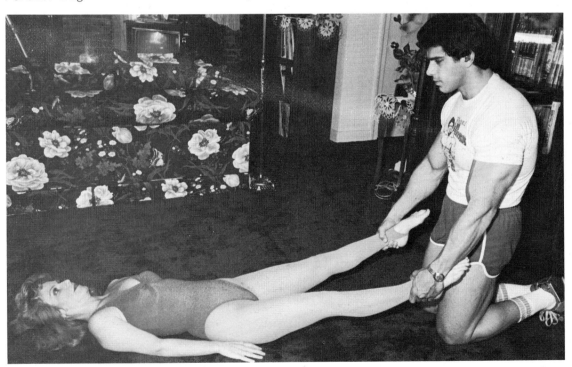

Partner Leg Abduction—finish.

to provide him with enough resistance for a good workout. Therefore, in our case he will usually just help me with such a workout whenever I am too busy with our business affairs to get to the gym. If you do these exercises with another woman, however, you should easily be able to give each other fairly strenuous workouts.

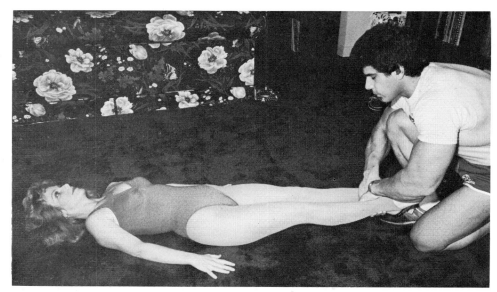

Partner Leg
Adduction—start.

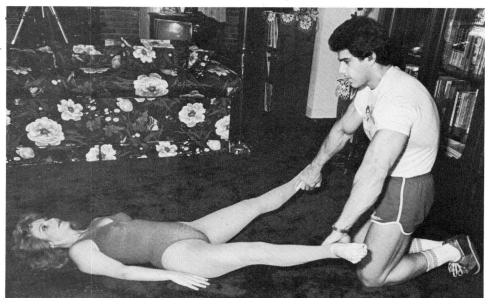

Partner Leg
Adduction—finish.

Partner Arm Curl—start.

Partner Arm Curl—finish.

Partner Exercise Routine

You now have 15 partner exercises to stress all of the major muscle groups of the body. These movements were chosen specifically to form a well-rounded routine. You simply need to do each exercise presented to give your full body a hard workout.

You should begin by doing 6–8 repetitions of each exercise (have your partner adjust his resistance to allow this number). Then gradually work up to 15 counts. Once you can do 15 repetitions, add a second set of 6–8 reps of each exercise. Two sets of 15

many families out bicycling as a group, often with a baby "papoosed" on the husband's back!

Ordinarily, a couple often has difficulty in coordinating workout schedules during the week, so weekends can be the best time for couple fitness activities. So during the week you can train on your own, and on the weekends with your husband or boyfriend.

Children and Fitness

You can give your children a tremendous advantage in life if you help them develop

counts in each movement will form quite a strenuous workout.

Partner Aerobics

Aerobic activities lend themselves well to partner and family involvement. Many couple run together, play racquetball or tennis, and bicycle together. And such activities as hiking and bicycling lend themselves well to family fitness. In fact, I've recently seen

an appreciation for the health and fitness lifestyle from the day they are born. As you become experienced with providing your family with good nutrition, you can easily come up with natural treats to replace the candy, soft drinks, and other sweets that most children seem to become addicted to at an early age. And, of course, you can supervise all of their meals at home to be sure that they are as nutritious and health-promoting as possible.

In terms of physical fitness, children can be included in family workouts from the time they are old enough to understand that exercising is fun. And children as young as 18–20 months of age can be taught to swim in special classes.

Actually, most children take to exercise like a duckling takes to the water. As soon as they see their parent exercising, they want to try it, too. And while very young children usually don't have full motor control of their bodies, they should be encouraged to mimic your exercises. Certainly, such exercises will not harm a growing young body, but don't expect a child to be too persistent in exercising. A young child's attention span is quite short, and almost anything can distract him or her from a workout.

When all is said and done, however, getting a child to exercise at a young age can hook him or her on the health and fitness lifestyle *for life!*

You can actually exercise very young children yourself. At the time my daughter Shanna Victoria reached the age of two months, I began putting her through a series of exercises each day in which I manipulated various parts of her body. These exercises greatly stimulated her physical development, and I am sure that they will do the same for any baby. On the following pages are descriptions and illustrations of each of these exercises. (Shanna Victoria was eight months old at the time these photos were taken.) Give them a try with your own baby!

Monkey Hang

This is an excellent movement for stretching all of the muscles of your baby's arms and torso. While you are seated, gently grasp your baby's hands and lift him upward. At the conclusion of this lift, your baby's arms will be straight and his body will be hanging downward from his arms.

Hold your baby in this position for 10 seconds at first and then gradually work up to 30 seconds. You'll be surprised at how much young babies enjoy hanging like this. Shanna Victoria laughs and kicks her legs vigorously whenever we do this exercise.

You will also be quite amazed at the strength of a baby's grip. By the age of three or four months a baby can grip a broomstick strongly enough with both hands to support his own body weight in a hanging position. If you use this gripping method with your baby, however, be sure to raise him over a soft surface, such as a couch cushion, and lift his feet only two or three inches from the cushion in case he falls.

Baby Sit-Ups

With assistance from his mother, any baby can do Sit-Ups to strengthen the muscles on the front of his abdomen. Teaching a baby to actually use abdominal strength to sit up, however, can take many weeks to accomplish. Begin the exercise by sitting at your baby's feet, with him lying on his back. Place your baby's toes gently under your thighs or positioned in such a manner that his legs are bent at approximately a 45-degree angle. Then grasp your baby's hands and simply pull gently on them to lift his shoulders from the floor. Your baby will automatically flex forward at the waist as you do this, until his torso is erect. Slowly lower him back to the start and repeat the movement for four or five counts. Gradually work up to 10–12 total repetitions. With time, your baby will learn that he can help himself sit up by contracting his stomach muscles. As this happens, you will need to pull upward less and less on his hands.

Baby Arm Supports

This simple exercise strengthens your baby's arm, shoulder, chest, stomach, and back muscles all at the same time. And at

Monkey Hang.

Baby Arm Support—start.

Baby Sit-Up—start.

Baby Sit-Up—finish.

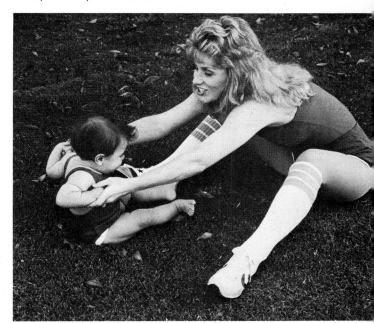

about two months of age, most babies can manage to do this movement quite well. As soon as you notice that your baby can push his torso upward by straightening his arms, or can hold his arms straight in this position, he is ready to do Baby Arm Supports. Sit behind your baby and pull his shoulders gently upward until he is supporting his torso on straight arms. Then gently pull up on his hips to shift a little of his body weight to his arms. With practice, you can eventually hold your baby by his feet as he supports all of his weight on his arms. Older babies will actually walk forward on their hands occasionally when in this position.

Assisted Walking

Long before your baby would ordinarily learn to walk on his own, you can support him for "walking" steps that will strengthen all of the muscles of his legs. The best way to support your child during this exercise is to hold him gently under his armpits. The only other secret to using this movement is to lean your baby slightly forward as you try to walk him. Even in very young babies this forward lean seems to cause a reflexive step ahead.

Assisted Walking.

Shoulder Articulation Movement

This exercise will stretch and strengthen your baby's shoulder, chest, and upper back muscles. Place your baby in a sitting position and sit behind him so you can support him in the sitting position with your legs as you perform the exercise. Gently grasp his hands and start with them next to your legs. Then slowly move his hands in semicircles directly out to the sides and upward until they touch directly above his head. Return his hands back along the same arcs to the starting point and repeat the movement for a total of 10 repetitions. Gradually work up to doing 20–25 counts of this exercise.

Arm Circle

This movement is a variation of the preceding exercise. Start in precisely the same position and raise your baby's arms out to a crucifix position. From there, slowly and gently move both hands in circles at arm's length from the body. Viewed from the side, your baby's hands will circle both clockwise and counterclockwise for 10–20 circles in each direction. Compared to the Shoulder Articulation Movement, this exercise stretches the chest and back muscles more, so be careful not to make your baby's hand circles too large in diameter at first.

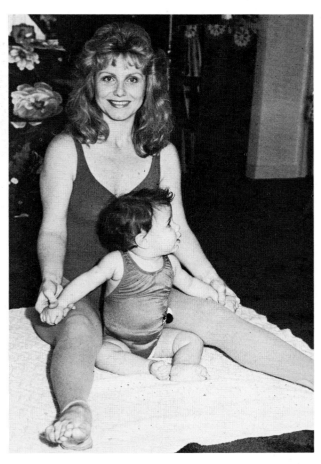

Shoulder Articulation Movement—start.

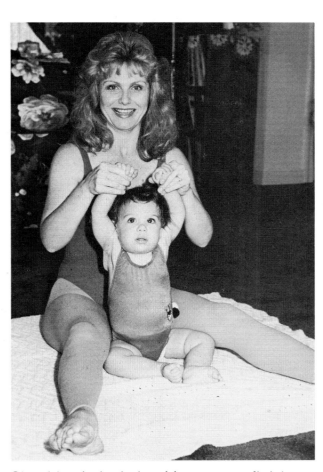

Shoulder Articulation Movement—finish.

Arm Circle—start.

Arm Circle—finish.

Trunk Twisting—start.

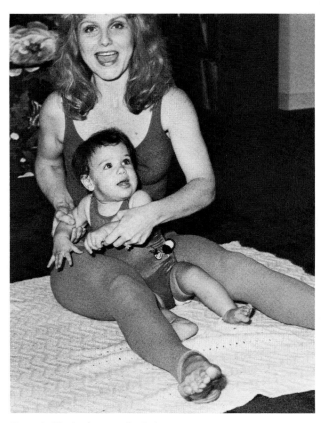

Trunk Twisting—finish.

Trunk Twisting

You can give your baby this exercise to strengthen and make more supple all of his torso muscles, particularly those of his lower back and at the sides of his waist. Start in exactly the same position as for Arm Circles, except that your baby's arms can be down at his sides throughout the movement. Grasp his shoulders and gently twist them a quarter-turn to the left. Then slowly and gently twist them back to the center line and do another quarter-turn to the right. Continue twisting your baby's shoulders back and forth for 10–15 counts to each side. Gradually work up to doing as many as 25–30 repetitions to each side.

Leg Crossover

Shanna Victoria gets a real kick out of this exercise, which stretches and strengthens virtually all of the muscles of her legs and torso. Start with your baby lying on his back. Imagine a line drawn perpendicular to his torso and through his hip joints. Grasp his feet and gently move the one in your right hand toward the left, across the midline of his body, and upward to touch the floor on the imaginary line through his hips. Let your baby's body twist and roll naturally as you do this. Return to the starting point and repeat the movement with the foot in your left hand in the opposite direction. Continue back and forth like this until you have done 8–10 counts to each side. Gradually work up to doing 20 counts to each side.

Chest and Back Articulation Movement

This exercise will directly stretch and

Chest and Back Articulation
Movement—start.

Chest and Back Articulation
Movement—finish.

strengthen your baby's chest and upper back muscles. Start sitting with your baby in the same position as for Arm Circles, holding his arms out to the sides. Keeping your baby's arms at this level and moving them parallel to the floor throughout the exercise, slowly move his hands forward until they touch each other directly in front of his chest. Then slowly move your baby's arms backward along the same arc and continue gently past the starting point as far behind his back as is comfortable for him. You should terminate this backward movement of your baby's arms the moment you sense any chest muscle tension retarding the movement. Move your baby's arms slowly back and forth between this rear position and the front position until you have done 8–10 repetitions in each direction. Gradually work up the number of counts to 20 in each direction.

Baby's Exercise Program

You can use this program with your baby daily if you like. For good results, however, you must do it a minimum of three nonconsecutive days per week (e.g., Mondays, Wednesdays, and Fridays, or Tuesdays, Thursdays, and Saturdays). Be sure not to exceed the recommended number of repetitions on any exercise.

If your baby has any physical abnormalities, he may not safely be able to do one or more of the recommended exercises. In such a case, it's essential that you check with your pediatrician to determine which exercises must be avoided. Take this book along with you so he can see the photos and read the descriptions of each exercise. This will prevent any possibility of a tragic misunderstanding.

I exercise Shanna Victoria on my own

exercise mat, which I further pad with a clean beach towel at each exercise session. I personally wear a leotard and tights for most of her exercise sessions, because I usually do my own workout shortly after hers. You can wear anything that is comfortable, however, and your baby can also wear whatever clothing he would wear in his own crib. If it's warm in the room, a diaper—or even no clothing at all—will be appropriate. On the other hand, when it's cooler, he would be better off wearing pajamas or a playsuit.

Above all, your baby's exercise periods should always be enjoyable and positive experiences. Your goal is to hook your children on the health and fitness lifestyle for life, not to discourage them from exercising in the future. So talk to your baby and smile a lot as you exercise him. And if he ever seems cranky or begins to cry during an exercise session, terminate it immediately and try again the next day. Most of the time, however, your baby will reward your efforts with smiles and happy sounds when you exercise him.

Family Fitness

No doubt you have heard the saying, "The family that prays together stays together." I am convinced that it is also true that "The family that *plays* together, stays together." Family recreational and fitness pursuits can greatly add to the enjoyment of life for every member of your family, just as the health and family fitness lifestyle has strengthened Lou, Shanna Victoria, and me as a family unit!

6

Energy Improvement

A huge number of American women seem to be plagued with low energy levels. After an eight-hour sit-down day at work, half of the women in America are too fatigued to go out for a night of dining and dancing. But this doesn't have to be the case! With the correct approach, you can have abundant energy at your command.

The Energy Cycle

Almost invariably a woman has poor energy levels because she is unhealthy, in poor physical condition, or both. Every healthy, fit woman whom I've known has been remarkably energetic. I've seen some women work 8–10 hours at a physically demanding job, work out quite strenuously for a couple of hours after work, and then enjoy a late date, with no shortage of energy.

Three primary factors contribute to this type of high energy level: (1) proper amounts of sleep and rest, (2) regular vigorous exercise, and (3) a healthy diet and the right food supplementation. Let's take each of these factors individually.

Sleep and Rest

The beauty of being healthy and in good physical condition is that you will invariably be able to sleep more soundly and efficiently than if you are out of shape and unhealthy. During the day I never run out of gas, and once I lie down to sleep I invariably fall asleep in only five or ten minutes. I sleep soundly for seven to eight hours, and when I wake up in the morning I am fully refreshed and anxious to face the new day.

Sleep and rest are important for full recuperation from daily physical and mental activity. So it's important to take periodic 10–15-minute rest breaks during the day to help recharge your run-down energy batteries. And it's necessary to allow yourself a full eight hours per night for sound sleep. Never let yourself go without sleep, regardless of how much work you have to do. You'll just run yourself down, and no one can work efficiently without sufficient sleep.

When you take your daily rest breaks, try to lie down on your back with a pillow under your knees and another one under your head. Completely empty your mind of stressful thoughts by thinking of a time during your life when you felt totally content and free of stress. Systematically relax your entire body, beginning with your feet and calves and proceeding up your body. Once you are fully relaxed, lie like this for five minutes before returning to continue your daily tasks.

Occasionally you will actually fall asleep while lying fully relaxed. Such a short nap can be particularly beneficial as a stress reducer, and it's the best way to fully recharge your energy batteries. I think that it's particularly good to nap in the late afternoon, a time during which most women experience their lowest energy levels.

Regular Exercise

If you're totally unfit, daily exercise will seem at first to force you into even greater depths of fatigue. But with only a week of following improved exercise habits and taking regular exercise, you'll notice that physical activity actually refreshes you. You will also discover yourself sleeping much better if you exercise every day.

Exercise tones your muscles and improves both your circulatory system and your metabolism. But above and beyond this, exercise helps reduce stress and tension, which can interfere with your sleep and relaxation patterns. Essentially it's impossible to maintain high levels of personal energy without regularly following a program of relatively strenuous exercise.

Chapters 4 and 5 were devoted to explanations of numerous types of exercise. There is enough variety in physical activity contained in those two chapters to keep anyone interested in working out. Aerobic exercise is particularly important in augmenting energy levels. Just be sure to work out every day, beginning easily and then gradually increasing the length of each training session. Once you have gotten yourself into good physical condition, you'll

be totally amazed at how much energy you have throughout the day!

Diet and Food Supplementation

In addition to the health-promoting diet that we discussed fully in Chapter 2, there are four food supplements that can help increase your reserves of personal energy. These are dessicated liver tablets, vitamin E capsules, chelated iron tablets, and tryptophan tablets.

Scientific experiments have proven that dessicated liver tablets significantly improve energy and endurance. In one experiment a group of laboratory rats was fed the normal lab rat diet, a second group was fed the lab rat diet plus synthetic B vitamins, and a third group was fed the lab rat diet plus all

of the dessicated liver each one wanted to eat. Then all three groups were placed in separate drums of water, from which they could not escape. The rats had to either swim or drown.

Group one swam an average of less than 20 minutes before drowning, while group two swam only slightly longer. Group three, however, swam three to four times as long as the other two groups before drowning, and several rats were still swimming vigorously when the experiment was terminated two hours later. The only dietary difference between group three and the other two groups of rats was the dessicated liver included in the group three rats' diets!

Vitamin E (as well as its unrefined form, wheat germ oil) has also been proven to improve energy and endurance. So has the use of chelated iron tablets, which are particularly valuable to menstruating women, who slough off red blood cells during their periods. Iron-rich blood has a high content of red blood cells, which allows for more efficient oxygen transfer in the bloodstream and hence promotes better energy and greater endurance.

Be careful that you don't take vitamin E and iron at the same meal, however. Taken together, they cancel out each other's effect. It's much better to take one supplement or the other, alternating the two food elements from meal to meal.

To improve energy with nutritional supplementation, take 10–20 dessicated liver tablets per day, 400–1,200 IU of vitamin E, and one or two chelated iron tablets or capsules per day (one ordinarily and two when menstruating). Then you will soon feel far more energetic throughout the day.

Tryptophan, one of the eight essential amino acids that make up proteins, is available in tablet form at health food stores. Tryptophan doesn't directly result in higher energy levels, but as a natural tranquilizer it helps you relax and get to sleep more quickly each night. Two or three tablets taken 30 minutes before bedtime will help you fall asleep as well as sleep much more deeply. I think you'll be amazed at how well tryptophan works. Women have told me that a tryptophan tablet is as good a tranquilizer as a Valium tablet.

Mental Attitude

I've personally found that my mental attitude directly dictates my energy levels. If I am depressed, I invariably feel low in energy. On the other hand, when I wake up feeling good about myself I have abundant energy reserves throughout the day.

Seeing yourself gradually improving your health and appearance, or effortlessly maintaining a good appearance and vibrant good health, is the best way to maintain a positive self-image. So, your self-image is dependent on regular exercise and a consistently good diet. You simply can't separate consistent exercise habits and a healthy diet from other factors influencing your energy levels.

Energy Thieves

There are several ways you can guarantee that your energy level will be low. But by recognizing and avoiding these "energy thieves," you can guarantee that you will have consistently abundant reserves of personal energy.

The first of these energy thieves is refined carbohydrates, particularly white sugar and white flour. Both of these foods consistently result in low energy levels, particularly if you are hypoglycemic (if you suffer from low blood sugar).

Hypoglycemia has reached epidemic proportions among Americans. Approximately half of all American men and women suffer from hypoglycemia, and approximately 25 percent of the population suffers from severe hypoglycemia.

Hypoglycemia causes depression, low energy levels, sharp and dramatic mood

swings, and symptoms of stress and anxiety. These symptoms can be minimized by avoiding refined carbohydrates and sticking largely to a high-protein diet.

It is relatively easy to determine if you suffer from hypoglycemia. Your family physician can give you a glucose tolerance test. This test is given in the morning after a period of fasting, and it doesn't involve any pain. You must fast the evening before the test to establish a sugar-depleted baseline blood sugar level. After taking a drink of concentrated glucose, the doctor will measure your blood sugar levels hourly for the next six hours. If your blood sugar shoots up and then falls equally as rapidly, you are hypoglycemic.

There are several hypoglycemia diets that will minimize the effects of the disorder on your body. Of course, following such a diet will give a hypoglycemic much greater energy levels. Most diets for hypoglycemia are centered around limiting—or completely eliminating—your consumption of refined carbohydrates, and particularly white sugar.

All types of drugs, even simple aspirin, are energy thieves. Obviously, amphetamines and other stimulants are counterproductive as far as personal energy levels are concerned. You might feel more energetic while under the influence of an upper, but taking one is equivalent to spending tomorrow today. You will be extremely low in energy the next day, tempting you to take another upper. Amphetamines, cocaine, and other stimulants are physically addicting.

Even coffee, chocolate, cola drinks, and other foods containing caffeine will adversely affect your energy levels. Caffeine first stimulates your energy levels, then drops them to new lows soon afterward. Tobacco and alcohol are similarly destructive. Other drugs that you should avoid include marijuana, painkillers of various types, and any type of tranquilizer.

Tranquilizers will help you artificially limit stress, as well as help you fall asleep each night. Valium is the most widely prescribed drug worldwide for these reasons, but in the long run Valium is an energy thief. There is also growing evidence that Valium is physically addicting. Certainly, there are millions of women around the world who are at least psychologically dependent on Valium.

Health and Energy

It's an unavoidable fact that your energy levels are directly dependent on your degree of mental and physical health. And your general health is dictated by your dietary and exercise habits. So, if you want to have abundant supplies of energy, you should maintain a healthy diet, exercise vigorously and regularly, and avoid energy thieves such as drugs, alcohol, and tobacco.

7

Uniquely Female Factors

Menstruation, pregnancy, childbirth, and menopause are functions unique to women. And I am happy to tell you that my health and fitness lifestyle is quite compatible with each of these natural functions. I can tell you this based on scientific studies, as well as my own personal experience with menstruation, pregnancy, and childbirth in relation to regular exercise and a healthy diet.

Menstruation

During my teenage years, when I was overweight and in very poor physical condition, I suffered every possible menstrual complication. I experienced such severe cramps that I dreaded the onset of each period. And once I was cramping, all I could think of was taking a pain pill and lying in bed until the cramps finally abated.

I also suffered from menstrual depression, breast tenderness, headaches, and periodic nausea. Believe me, I've suffered as severely as any woman from menstrual complications. But today I am completely free of such problems, and I haven't experienced any of them for years.

I firmly believe that menstrual irregularities are caused, or at least aggravated, by a poor diet and deficient exercise habits. Within two months of adopting a health and fitness lifestyle, I was free from menstrual problems. If you suffer from these irregularities, you too can be free from them within a few short weeks. All you need to do is adopt a health and fitness lifestyle.

Very few physically active women have period-related difficulties. All types of exercise will relieve tension, but in my experience aerobic exercise that involves the legs is most beneficial in relieving menstrual irregularities. Jogging, bicycling, and swimming are particularly beneficial, as is an occasional aerobic dance class. Merely exercising for a few days before the onset of your period can help reduce menstrual problems, but you will experience a complete remission of such problems if you can exercise regularly throughout the month.

Cramps and depression are often caused by mineral deficiencies before and during the menstrual cycle. Merely following a healthy, balanced diet will relieve some of these problems, but through proper food supplementation you can drastically reduce cramps and depression. You should take a chelated mutiple mineral tablet twice per day for a week prior to the onset of your period, during your period, and for two or three days following the cessation of your period.

If normal mineral supplementation doesn't sufficiently relieve your menstrual problems, you should also include four individual chelated minerals in tablet form each day for the same period of time that you take the multiple minerals. The individual minerals you should take are calcium, iron, magnesium, and potassium. With this full supplementation schedule, a healthy and balanced diet, and regular exercise, your menstrual problems will soon be a thing of the past.

Pregnancy and Childbirth

Having recently had my first baby with a total absence of problems, after which I quickly made a complete return to my pre-pregnancy appearance and physical condition, I can speak with authority on eating and exercising while pregnant, the effect of a health and fitness lifestyle on childbirth, and how to rapidly regain a sexy appearance after giving birth. I also have read numerous scientific studies on the relationship of diet and exercise to pregnancy and childbirth.

There is a direct relationship between a woman's physical condition and her chances of avoiding the ills often associated with pregnancy, as well as the possibility of childbirth complications. Physically active and healthy women seldom suffer from fatigue, back pains, or excessive weight gain during pregnancy. They have easy labors and experience far fewer complications in childbirth. And once they give birth they quickly get back into good shape.

Compared to friends who have had first babies, my pregnancy was a breeze, because I was in very good physical condition before becoming pregnant. Then I exercised regularly during my pregnancy and ate only good foods. As a result, my weight gain was quite normal, and I never ran out of energy. In fact, I conducted my full work load each day up to the day I gave birth.

My baby was quite large (12 pounds), and my labor was relatively long as a result. My doctor later told me that I would no doubt have had to have a Caesarean section rather than a natural childbirth if I'd been in lesser physical condition. I think any woman would prefer to give birth normally, so my workouts and dietary practices allowed me a great joy that I wouldn't otherwise have had.

With your obstetrician's direction, you can exercise regularly throughout your pregnancy. I actually attended organized exercise classes for pregnant women, but you can exercise at home by pedaling a stationary bicycle and doing the following exercises.

Lower Back/Hamstring Stretch

Stand erect with your feet set about three feet apart. Your toes should point slightly outward, and you should keep your legs straight throughout the movement. Bend slowly and gently forward and to the right side and place your hands flat on the floor near your right foot. Hold this gently stretched position for 10–15 seconds. Gradually build up to about 30 seconds in each stretched position. Stand erect and then slowly bend toward your left leg and place your hands flat on the floor near your left foot. Hold this gently stretched position for 10–15 seconds, gradually building up to holding the stretch for about 30 seconds. This movement stretches and strengthens the muscles at the back of your thighs and your lower back muscles.

Lower Back/Hamstring Stretch.

Seated Side Stretch.

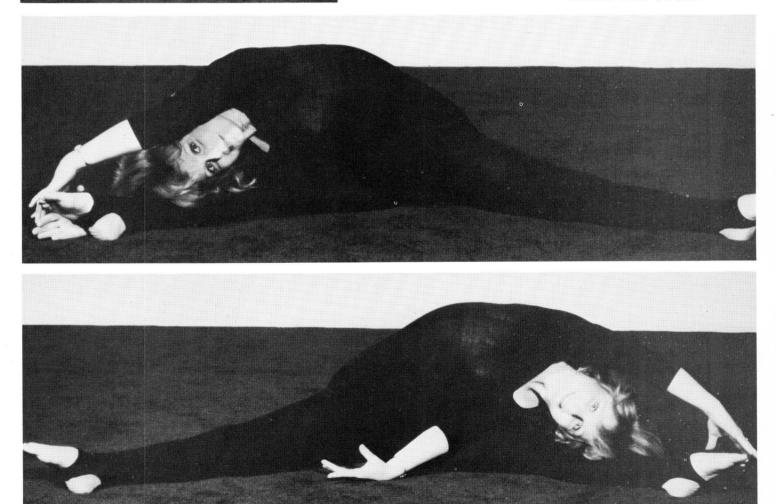

Seated Side Stretch

Sit on a mat on the floor and place your legs as far apart as possible (see illustrations). You must keep your legs straight throughout the movement. Start sitting with your torso erect. Lean your torso toward your right leg, grasping your right ankle with both hands and pulling your torso gently toward your leg. Hold this stretched position for 10–15 seconds and gradually work up to holding the stretch for 30 seconds. Do an equal amount of stretching toward your left leg. As an alternative, you can do the stretch freehand without pulling your torso down to your leg (as illustrated). This movement stretches your hamstrings, inner thigh muscles, lower back, and all of the muscles along the sides of your torso.

Kneeling Jazz Kick

Kneel on the floor and anchor your hands to the mat as illustrated. You should also anchor your right knee to the floor. Bend your left leg and flex it up under your torso (as illustrated) as far as is comfortable. Then slowly arch your back and extend your leg as high as comfortably possible to the rear. Pause in this top position for a moment, then return to the starting position and repeat the movement for the desired number of repetitions. Do an equal number of repetitions using your right leg. At a maximum, you can do 25–30 repetitions with each leg. This movement strengthens and tones all of your hip, back, and leg muscles.

Knee Pull-In

Lie on your back with your hands under your buttocks as illustrated. With your legs straight and pressed together, raise your legs upward until your feet are about six inches from the floor. From that basic starting position, slowly bend your legs while simul-taneously pulling your knees gently in toward your abdomen as fully as possible with comfort. Slowly return to the starting position by straightening your legs. Repeat for up to 30 consecutive slow movements. This exercise tones and strengthens all of the muscles on the front of your abdomen.

Lying Leg Swing

Lie on your right side and support your torso in position using one of the two alternative arm positions illustrated. Slightly bend your right leg to help steady your torso during the movement. Raise your straight left leg upward directly to the side until your foot is 6–8 inches from the floor. Keeping your left leg at that level, slowly move your leg forward as far as is comfortable. Slowly return to the starting position and repeat the movement for up to 30 consecutive repetitions. Do an equal number of repetitions with your right leg while lying on the floor on your left side. This movement tones and strengthens all of the muscles on the sides of your hips and the outsides of your thighs.

Hurdler's Stretch

Sit on the floor and extend your left leg straight out in front of your torso. Keep your left leg straight throughout the movement. Bend your right leg and tuck it behind your hip as illustrated. Start with your torso erect. Lean slowly and gently forward and toward your left leg. Grasp your left ankle to increase the range of motion in the stretch. Hold the fully stretched position for 10–15 seconds and slowly build up to holding it for approximately 30 seconds. Do an equal amount of stretching with your right leg straight and your left leg folded behind your hip. This exercise stretches and tones all of the muscles at the sides of your torso, at the back of your thighs, and on your inner thighs.

Kneeling Jazz Kick—start, left; finish, below.

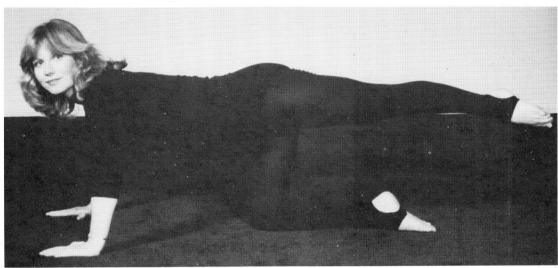

Supported Lunge

Start standing fully erect. Step directly forward about 2½–3 feet with your left foot. Keeping your right leg relatively straight, bend your left leg as fully as possible. Slowly incline your torso forward until you can support your upper body on straight arms as illustrated. Hold this stretched position for 10–15 seconds, then slowly work up to holding the stretch for 30 seconds. Reverse your foot position and do an equal amount of stretching with your right foot forward. This movement stretches and strengthens virtually every major muscle group of your body, but particularly those of your legs and hips.

Seated Bicycle

Lie on your back on a mat and support your torso on your arms as illustrated. From this position gently lift your legs from the floor and then slowly move them in circles above the floor as if you were pedaling a bicycle. Continue the movement for up to 30 repetitions with each leg. This exercise tones and strengthens all of the muscles of your thighs and frontal abdomen.

Knee Pull-In—start, above; finish, right.

Lying Leg Swing—
start, above; finish,
right.

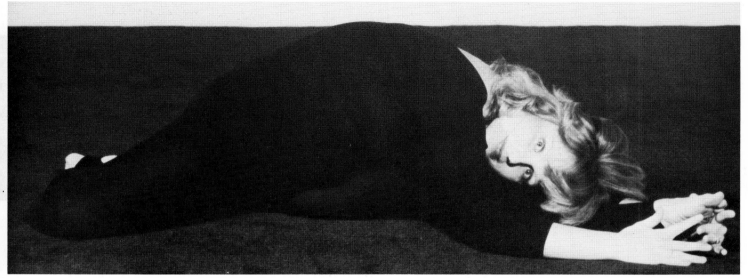

Hurdler's
Stretch
(above).

Supported
Lunge
(left).

Seated
Bicycle
(below).

V-Sitting Stretch

Sit on a mat on the floor and spread your legs as wide as possible. You must keep your legs straight throughout this stretch. Slowly lean forward, supporting the weight of your torso on your arms. Hold a fully stretched position for 10–15 seconds, gradually working up until you can hold the stretch for about 30 seconds. The wider you spread your legs at the start of the movement, the greater the degree of stretch you will feel on the back of your thighs and inner thighs. The more you lean forward during the stretch, the more you will stretch your lower back and hamstrings.

Side Leg Raise

Lie on your right side on a mat and support your upper torso on your right arm as illustrated. Keeping your left leg held straight, slowly raise it in a semicircle from a position touching your right thigh to as high a position as possible. You can actually grasp your leg as I am doing to increase the range of motion. Slowly return your leg to the starting position and repeat the movement for up to 30 counts. Be sure to do an equal number of repetitions with your right leg while lying on your left side. This exercise tones and strengthens all of the muscles on the sides of your hip and outsides of your thighs.

Body Bridge

Lie on your back on a mat placed on the floor. Place your arms down at your sides with your hands about a foot away from your hips and leave your arms in this position throughout the movement. Pull your heels toward your buttocks until they are about a foot away from your buttocks. Keeping your feet in this position, contract your hip and lower back muscles to pull your buttocks off the mat to the position

illustrated. Hold this position for a count of two and then slowly lower yourself back to the floor. Begin with four or five repetitions and slowly work up to doing 15 counts. This exercise tones and strengthens the muscles of your hips, buttocks, and lower back.

You can do this exercise program once per day. It should take no more than about 20 minutes to complete. If you feel particularly tense, you might find it beneficial to do the program twice per day, once in the morning and once at night.

It is also important that you continue to do some type of aerobic movement under the direction of your physician. In my experience the two easiest and safest forms of aerobic exercise while pregnant are swimming and pedaling a stationary bicycle.

Throughout your pregnancy you should continue to follow a healthy diet. It's impossible to maintain perfect health and optimum physical condition without watching your nutritional intake. Exercise alone won't do the job for you.

Following childbirth you will find it far easier to get back to normal if you've maintained great physical condition throughout your pregnancy. I've seen many women let themselves go while pregnant, then have to spend two or three months just getting into good enough physical condition to begin exercising hard enough to regain their pre-pregnancy appearance. By the time three months had passed in my case, I was in better shape and looked better than ever before!

For the first three or four weeks after childbirth, you'll lose weight rather rapidly, because your body retains water during a pregnancy. Such water is relatively easy to lose. Past this point, however, accumulated body fat will gradually dissipate only as a result of your everyday healthy approach to diet and exercise. If you remained in good condition during pregnancy, you will be back to normal in three months or less after giving birth.

V-Sitting
Stretch
(above).

Side Leg
Raise (left).

Body Bridge
(below).

Menopause

Hundreds of thousands of American women each year suffer from maladies associated with menopause, and in most cases they do so needlessly. They suffer from drastic and abrupt mood swings and especially from depression. They endure various physical pains, and they endure energy lows.

Did you know that in more primitive societies that encourage women to stay physically active as they mature such menopausal problems are virtually unknown? As with menstrual irregularities, menopausal symptoms can be greatly relieved, even eliminated completely, through attention to regular exercise habits and a healthy diet.

During menopause a woman's hormone balances are gradually changed, and this is what causes mood swings, depression, and other symptoms associated with "change of life." By exercising regularly and vigorously, with emphasis on aerobic activity, you can smooth out these hormonal changes.

A healthy, balanced diet liberally supplemented with chelated multiple minerals and B-complex vitamins can further mellow hormone-related mood swings. And by combining this diet with regular exercise, you can pass through menopause with a minimum of difficulty and discomfort.

Women and Health

What I've been trying to say in this chapter is that I'm overjoyed to be a woman who has adopted a health and fitness lifestyle. Regular exercise and a healthy diet go well with being a woman, and when combined they will greatly reduce—even eliminate—potential problems related to such uniquely female physiological functions as menstruation, pregnancy, childbirth, and menopause. Give the health and fitness lifestyle a try!

8

A Personal
Lifestyle

To tie up any loose ends left by the preceding seven chapters, this chapter includes questions and answers regarding how I have personally applied the principles outlined in this book to my own lifestyle. The questions and answers making up this chapter have been edited and extracted from a lengthy interview conducted by Bill Reynolds, editor-in-chief of *Muscle & Fitness* magazine. These remarks are an accurate representation of how I feel about each of the questions presented, and I am sure that you will find my answers helpful in solving your own health- and fitness-related problems.

Q: *How overweight were you when you discovered how to diet and exercise?*

A: I was 5'2" tall and weighed 150 pounds, which is overweight by any definition. I wore a size 16 dress, while today I wear a size five. It took me three months to lose enough weight to appear normal. I was sure to exercise every day, and I cut back considerably on my total food intake. I ate breakfast, lunch, and dinner, but only small amounts of food at each meal. Other than a

raw carrot, I ate no snacks. I also avoided sugar in my diet. I ate protein and vegetables, one slice of bread per day, and drank a half glass of milk each day. I would say that I ate about 900 calories per day.

Q: *What's your personal health and fitness philosophy?*

A: I don't walk when I can run, and I don't sit when I can stand. If you follow this type of philosophy, you're always looking for ways to be more active and hence to burn off more calories. Also, I don't drink my calories. If you drink alcohol, juices, or a lot of milk, it is very easy to drink 3,000 calories per day that you would otherwise avoid.

Q: *Obviously, your husband Lou was already involved in exercising and watching his diet. But what if a woman has a boyfriend or husband who isn't? How would she get him involved in her program?*

A: I firmly believe that exercise is something to be enjoyed, and it is something to share with your mate. I would approach someone who isn't involved with exercise

and a healthy diet and say, "Let's be a little closer. Let's have fun together." I think that approach will always be successful.

Q: *How does your program affect your energy levels?*

A: My energy is incredible compared to when I was overweight. A healthy diet and regular training are vital for energy production, and merely feeling good about yourself is a tremendous energy booster.

Q: *Would your program be suitable for use by diabetics?*

A: Yes. I have a medical background, and along with giving them a special diet, physicians tell diabetics to exercise regularly. So, I'm sure that a health and fitness lifestyle would be applicable to a diabetic woman.

Q: *Isn't it painful to exercise so much?*

A: There's a little pain involved when you fatigue yourself, but it's actually somewhat pleasurable, because you know that it means you're making progress. And the better your physical condition becomes, the less it hurts.

Q: *Is your health and fitness lifestyle applicable to all women? It would seem that the only women who could follow your program are younger girls and students, both of whom have considerable free time.*

A: I believe that any woman, regardless of how busy she feels she might be, can profit from a program of sensible diet and regular exercise. It doesn't take any more time to prepare a healthy diet for yourself and your family than it does to prepare a

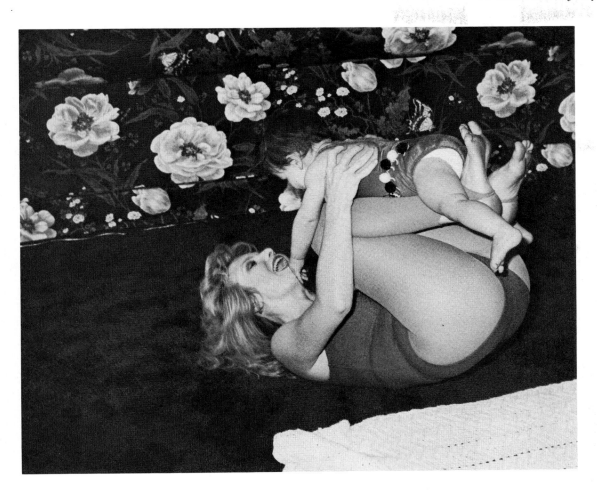

diet of junk foods. And when you are physically fit and healthy you can work and sleep so efficiently that you will more than make up in time savings at work the 30–45 minutes you will spend exercising each day. At 32 years of age, I'm no longer a teenager, and I work very hard 8–10 hours per day caring for my home and family and managing my husband's acting career. Still, I thrive on my health and fitness lifestyle. In fact, I couldn't put in the long hours working that I do without following a healthy diet and exercising every day.

If you took a random sampling of all the women who follow a health and fitness program similar to my own, you would discover that these women form a representative cross section of American society. The sample would include younger women and more mature women, students and housewives, secretaries and professional women, single women and married women with families, even women who are physically handicapped. I can't conceive of a woman who wouldn't benefit from following the health and fitness lifestyle that I recommend.

Q: *Would it be appropriate for a woman of 60 or 65 to adopt a health and fitness lifestyle?*

A: Yes, definitely. Regardless of a woman's age, she can benefit enormously from switching to a healthy diet and exercising regularly. More mature women won't be able to exercise as vigorously as a teenager, and thus won't progress as fast in achieving physical fitness, but a health and fitness lifestyle will add greatly to an older woman's quality of life. I know several women in their seventies who exercise every day and enjoy life more than many teenagers. If you've been physically inactive for more than a year, I would suggest that you have a physical examination before beginning to exercise regularly, however.

At the lower end of the age scale, my daughter is eight months old and I exercise with her every day, much to her glee. We've actually been exercising together since she was five months old. She's never tasted junk foods like refined sugar, and I hope that she never does. Believe me, you've never seen a healthier and more active baby!

Q: *Can a woman expect very quick results if she follows your dietary and exercise recommendations?*

A: Yes, noticeable results can be seen in two weeks, and within three months she can change her health and appearance dramatically enough to startle friends and relatives who haven't seen her during the transformation. Women who are overweight to begin with will be able to lose 20–30 pounds of body fat in three months, which remarkably changes their appearance. Even women of normal weight will firm their bodies and develop a healthy glow to their skin that only good living can produce. As you progress with your own health and fitness lifestyle, you will soon discover that beauty truly comes from the inside out.

Q: *Some women seem to be in good physical condition, except for flab on the backs of their upper arms, or on their upper thighs. Can you offer these women any hope?*

A: I once suffered from both of these problems, and would soon suffer from them again if I relaxed my exercise program and began to eat the wrong foods. With sufficient time following a health and fitness way of life, you shouldn't have extraneous fat bulges anywhere on your body.

Q: *From your answer to the previous question it almost seems like a woman will become a slave for life to her diet and exercise regimen. Can't this become a burden?*

A: On the contrary, the health and fitness lifestyle is such a joy that any woman would be reluctant to give it up. You get to the point where you actually prefer healthy food to junk foods. And you become so "positively addicted" to daily exercise that you won't feel completely comfortable if you miss a workout. Still, when traveling to personal appearances overseas with my husband I've gone a week or two without appreciable exercise and on a bad diet without regressing in my health or physical fitness.

Now I've gotten to the point where I am easily able to maintain my diet and exercise program while traveling. I eat a lot of salads and broiled fish in restaurants, and Lou and I do our couple exercises in the hotel room. We've even gone out to find a spa for weight workouts when traveling. Regardless of where you travel, you can at least take a 20- to 30-minute run each day.

Q: *Many women are afraid that they'll get fat again if they are forced to stop working out. Do you think that this can happen?*

A: Even if a woman stops working out, there's no reason why she would also have to revert to an unhealthy diet. And even without exercising regularly, she can keep looking slender merely by following a good diet. She won't be as physically fit as she would be if she still exercised, but a woman will still be healthier and have a better physical appearance than if she had never exercised or adopted a good diet.

When you're in perfect shape, you have more muscle tissue than when you don't work out. Many men and women believe that muscle will turn to fat if you don't work out, but this is a myth. Any muscle that isn't exercised will slowly shrink in size, but it's physiologically impossible for muscle tissue to turn to fat.

tancy of less than 10 years. With progressive exercise, such a short life expectancy can be extended significantly. And, perhaps more importantly, regular exercise improves the quality of life of any physically handicapped individual.

Q: *You mentioned weight training. Many men and women are afraid that weight training will make them muscle-bound, that it'll ruin their golf game, or whatever.*

A: This contention is exactly the opposite of the truth. As long ago as 1950, scientists determined that weight training actually makes the body's muscles more flexible. And there are mountains of evidence that weight training improves athletic ability. Of all those factors blending to make a champion athlete—such as speed, strength, balance, skill, a good mental attitude, experience, etc.—the easiest quality to improve is strength. And with improvements in strength often come dramatic improvements in athletic performance. If weight training was detrimental to athletic performance, you would not see so many athletes training with weights. And yet there are numerous athletes in every sport who use weights. In some sports virtually all athletes do weight workouts.

Q: *Earlier, you mentioned that exercise would be good for handicapped women. Would this include a paraplegic woman?*

A: Yes, it would. Any woman who has at least partial use of her arms and/or legs can do weight training exercises. The beauty of weight training is that it is very selective. There are numerous exercises that key in specifically on single muscle groups. If a woman has use of only her arms and shoulders, she can still do weight training movements for these two body parts. And overall she will be much healthier from doing these limited weight training workouts than if she remained inactive. Inactivity leads to early death. Men who received spinal injuries in the Vietnam War and were confined to wheelchairs had a life expec-

Q: *Many women would contend that your program might make their bodies lose their femininity. How would you answer such an assertion?*

A: I think I'm a good example of evidence contrary to this belief. Do I look unfeminine? I don't think you'd find many men or women who would agree with that statement. And yet I train vigorously with weights three times per week.

Actually, it's impossible for a woman to lose her femininity through vigorous exercise. To develop masculine muscles you would need a high level of the male hormone *testosterone*. Women do secrete a small amount of testosterone, but nothing near the amount that would be required to look masculine. Additionally, we secrete large amounts of the feminizing hormone *estrogen,* which easily overwhelms the effect of any testosterone we produce. In point of fact, any muscle tissue that we gain will appear on our bodies as feminine curves.

Q: *Can a woman with a bad back follow your exercise program?*

A: Yes, and the exercise—particularly the stretching movements—will improve her back condition. I spent three very miserable years in my early twenties with a back so painful that I often had to spend entire days in bed. The doctors my family consulted forbade me to exercise with the fear that it would further injure my back. Finally, in despair I began to exercise every day. Within two or three weeks my back condition was a thing of the past, and I have had no problems with it for more than 10 years.

If you do have a chronically sore back, I'd recommend that you concentrate on doing the stretching program outlined in this book. You should also do the Hyperextension movement described in the section on couple exercises. Do the stretching five or six days per week, and do your Hyperextensions three nonconsecutive days each week until your sore back disappears.

Q: *I've heard women complain that they can't exercise because they're afraid that the added physical activity will increase their appetite. Can you comment on this?*

A: Actually, hard exercise is an effective appetite supressant. For an hour or two after a hard workout, you won't be hungry, and you certainly won't eat any more food because you exercise. You will actually burn off surplus calories while working out, so the net effect will be one of body fat loss, not a weight gain.

Q: *Is it a good idea to continue exercising while pregnant?*

A: As long as your obstetrician approves

of your exercise program, you won't harm yourself while exercising. In fact, you'll find that you have fewer pregnancy complications and an easier labor if you stay in good physical condition while pregnant.

Another factor to consider is that you will make a faster comeback after giving birth if you stay physically active and in good physical condition while pregnant. I was back to 90 percent of my prepregnancy appearance and body weight six weeks after giving birth. And three months after giving birth I was in better overall condition and had a better physical appearance than before I became pregnant.

Q: *Can a woman profitably exercise while she is menstruating?*

A: Yes, and she'll have far fewer cramps and other menstrual problems if she does. I know from bitter personal experience that a woman who is having menstrual cramps just wants to lie in bed and sleep it off, usually under the influence of a heavy painkiller. With regular exercise, I no longer have menstrual complications. Every woman I know who is physically active is relatively free from menstrual cramping. I think that regular exercise and a healthy diet will minimize menstrual problems, as well as minimize the problems many women undergo during menopause. Menopausal problems are a phenomenon of modern civilization. Historically, you don't find them in societies that were primitive enough to keep women physically active.

Q: *You've said that exercise and diet will solve an obese woman's problem and normalize her weight. Will exercise and a good diet help a severely underweight woman normalize her weight, too?*

A: Yes, with weight training and an increased-calorie diet, an underweight woman can normalize her body weight and physical appearance within a year. A woman who is underweight should increase her caloric intake by 10–15 percent and train with relatively low repetitions (6–8 reps on an average) on the weight training program recommended in this book.

Q: *Is your program expensive to follow?*
A: It could be if you invest in designer

warm-up suits and expensive spa memberships, but under normal circumstances you might even make a net savings on my program over what it normally costs you to live. Healthy foods cost less than eating junk foods at a fast-food restaurant, and you needn't make any significant equipment investments. Even if you purchase a weight set, it won't set you back more than about $50.

Q: *How much time is involved in following your program?*
A: The food preparation is the same as what you now put in, and the exercise will take no more than 30–45 minutes per day. As I mentioned earlier, though, you will more than make up for this time expenditure in improved work efficiency once you are in good physical condition.

Q: *Is it possible just to exercise or just diet without involving yourself with the other factor?*
A: Yes, but a woman won't make as much progress just exercising or just dieting as she will make if she exercises *and* watches her diet.

Q: *Have you ever had any regrets about adopting your present lifestyle?*
A: No, and I don't think that I will ever have such regrets. I have never felt better than I do now, and I seem to get more healthy and achieve better physical condition with each passing year. There is nothing in my experience that would cause me to abandon my present lifestyle. I share it with my entire family, and it has brought us all closer together. I simply wouldn't feel complete as a woman and as a human being if I didn't eat the way I presently do or if I failed to exercise regularly. And anyone who has adopted my lifestyle has felt just as good as I do. The effects of such a way of life are simply unbelievable to the average woman!

Appendix 1:

Caloric Expenditure, Common Physical Activities

Activity	Calories Burned
Running (10 mph)	450
Bicycling (15 mph)	300
Cross-Country Skiing (10 mph)	300
Handball/Squash	300
Stationary Bicycling (10 mph)	250
Singles Tennis	200
Downhill Skiing	175
Aerobic Dance Class	150
Volleyball	140
Softball	135
Weight Training	130
Walking (2 mph)	130

Note: Caloric expenditure values are based on 30 minutes of continuous activity and can vary 5–10 percent above or below the values states. These variances are a function of body weight and degree of vigor with which each activity is pursued.

Appendix 2:

Food Calorie Charts

HIGH-CALORIE FOODS TO AVOID

Calories	Food (serving size)
107	Cheese, American (1 oz.)
103	Cheese, Blue (1 oz.)
215	Cheese, Cottage (1 cup)
105	Cheese, Cream (1 oz.)
106	Cheese, Monterey Jack (1 oz.)
104	Cheese, Muenster (1 oz.)
110	Cheese, Parmesan (1 oz.)
245	Cheese, Ricotta (1 cup)
315	Cream (1 cup)
75	Eggs, whole (one medium)
159	Milk, whole (1 cup)
980	Milk, condensed, sweetened (1 cup)
270	Sherbet (1 cup)
230	Yogurt, low-fat with fruit (8 oz.)
400	Cake, frosted (small wedge)
145	Chocolate (1 oz.)
55	Cookies (one average)
125	Doughnut (one average)
65	Honey (1 tablespoon)
50	Jams and Jellies (1 teaspoon)
410	Pie, Apple (one average slice)
670	Pie, Pecan (one average slice)
390	Pudding, Chocolate (1 cup)
770	Sugar (1 cup)
50	Syrup, Maple (1 tablespoon)
50	Syrup, Corn (1 tablespoon)
230	Fruit, Dried (1 cup)
335	Avocado (one average)
225	Fruit, canned with sugar (1 cup)

275	Dates (10 medium)
1400	Beef (1 pound)
1400	Hot Dogs (1 pound)
3000	Pork (1 pound)
1600	Sausage (1 pound)
850	Almonds (1 cup)
915	Brazil Nuts (1 cup)
785	Cashews (1 cup)
855	Hazel Nuts (1 cup)
840	Peanuts, Roasted (1 cup)
90	Peanut Butter (1 tablespoon)
750	Pecans (1 cup)
875	Sesame Seeds (1 cup)
815	Sunflower Seeds (1 cup)
785	Walnuts (1 cup)
125	Cooking Oil (1 tablespoon)
75	Salad Dressing, Blue Cheese (1 tablespoon)
75	Salad Dressing, Caesar (1 tablespoon)
75	Salad Dressing, Green Goddess (1 tablespoon)
85	Salad Dressing, Italian (1 tablespoon)
80	Salad Dressing, Thousand Island (1 tablespoon)
665	Beans, Dry Pinto (1 cup)
230	Beans, Red Kidney, Canned (1 cup)
235	Soybeans (1 cup)
330	Wine, Sweet (1 cup)
205	Wine, Dry (1 cup)
105	Beer (1 cup)
110	Soft Drink, Fruit-Flavored (1 cup)
700	Barley, Dry (1 cup)
120	Bread, Enriched (one average slice)
100	Cereal, Dry (1 cup)
425	Cornmeal (1 cup)
55	Crackers, Graham (one large)
115	Muffins (one average)
180	Pizza (small slice)
180	Rolls, Danish (one)
535	Tapioca, Dry (1 cup)
220	Waffle, Plain (one)

LOW-CALORIE FOODS TO EAT

Calories	Food (serving size)
80	Cheese, Mozzarella, Nonfat (1 oz.)
17	Egg White (one large)
85	Milk, Nonfat (1 cup)
445	Abalone (1 lb.)
470	Bass (1 lb.)
465	Catfish (1 lb.)
355	Cod (1 lb.)

420	Crab, Steamed (1 lb.)
360	Flounder (1 lb.)
360	Haddock (1 lb.)
455	Halibut (1 lb.)
415	Lobster (1 lb.)
300	Oysters (1 cup)
430	Perch (1 lb.)
420	Pike (1 lb.)
365	Scallops (1 lb.)
420	Red Snapper (1 lb.)
255	Tuna, Water-Packed (1 cup)
95	Apple (one medium)
90	Berries (1 cup)
105	Cantaloupe (one average)
90	Cherries (1 cup)
80	Grapefruit (one average)
40	Honeydew Melon (large slice)
60	Orange (one average)
40	Peach (one medium)
120	Pear (one average)
80	Pineapple (1 cup)
20	Strawberries (1 cup)
150	Watermelon (large slice)
300	Chicken, Skinned Breast (1 pound)
380	Turkey, Skinned Breast (1 pound)
2	Vinegar (1 tablespoon)
55	Soup, Beef Vegetable (1 cup)
50	Soup, Chicken with Rice (1 cup)
trace	Spices, Most
30	Vegetables, Most (1 cup)
8	Vegetables, Salad Greens (1 cup)
20	Mushrooms, Raw (1 cup)
120	Potato, Baked (one large, unbuttered)
175	Rice, Brown, Cooked (1 cup)

Glossary

Aerobic Exercise Any low-intensity type of movement that can be carried out continuously for extended periods of time within the body's ability to provide oxygen to the working muscles as fast as it is used up. *Aerobic* means literally "with oxygen." Typical aerobic activities include jogging, dancing, bicycling, swimming, walking, and roller skating.

Anaerobic Exercise This is a high-intensity form of exercise that burns oxygen at a rate faster than it can be supplied by the body to the working muscles. Such a high rate of oxygen consumption quickly develops a severe oxygen debt, forcing you to terminate the exercise session. Typical anaerobic activities include fast running and weight training with little or no rest between sets.

Bar The steel shaft forming the handle of a barbell or dumbbell. The bar of most dumbbells is 12–14 inches long, while barbell bars vary in length from four to seven feet. The weight of this bar must be taken into consideration when adding plates to form a required exercise poundage. Generally speaking, bars weigh approximately five pounds per foot of length.

Barbell Consisting of a bar, sleeve, collars, and plates, this is the basic piece of equipment for weight training. Barbells can be either adjustable (allowing the weights to be changed) or fixed (with the plates welded or otherwise permanently fastened into place on the bar).

Bodybuilding A type of weight training in which the primary objective is to change the form or appearance of one's body. Often bodybuilding can be a competitive sport for both men and women.

Collar The cylindrical metal fastener that holds barbell or dumbbell plates in position on the bar. There are inside collars and outside collars, both of which are held in position on the bar by means of a set screw or special clamp.

Dumbbell This is merely a short-handled

barbell, intended primarily for use in one hand. A dumbbell has all of the other characteristics of a barbell.

Exercise Each individual movement done in a weight training program (e.g., a Bench Press or a Squat). This is also sometimes called a *movement.*

Flexibility A suppleness of the body's joints and muscles. Flexibility is developed by regularly following a comprehensive course of stretching exercises.

Food Supplements Concentrated forms of protein, vitamins, and minerals taken as an adjunct to the normal diet. Food supplements provide the body with a superior form of nutritional intake.

Intensity The amount of actual work done by a single muscle or the entire body during an exercise or an entire workout. Intensity is normally increased in weight training by adding weight to the bar or machine being used or by increasing the number of repetitions done for an exercise. In other activities, intensity is usually increased by packing more total work into a uniform time period.

Nutrition The entire spectrum of nutrients taken into the body each day. Nutrition consists of the normal everyday diet and the food supplements you consume. Optimum health is impossible without a high quality of daily nutritional intake.

Physical Fitness Physical fitness means a high level of cardiorespiratory efficiency, physical strength, joint and muscle flexibility, and psychological well-being.

Plates The flat cast-iron or vinyl-covered concrete discs that are fitted on the ends of a barbell or dumbbell bar to make up the training poundage required for a particular exercise.

Repetition Each individual complete cycle of a weight training exercise (e.g., the full bending and straightening of the arms in a Bench Press). This term is often abbreviated to *rep.* Normally, several repetitions (usually 6–12) are done of each exercise in a training program.

Rest Interval The pause of 30–90 seconds between sets of a weight training workout. A rest interval is necessary to allow the working muscle to recuperate partially before a subsequent set is initiated.

Routine The complete program of exercises done on an individual training day. This is also called a *program* or a *schedule.*

Set A distinct grouping of repetitions of a particular weight training exercise, after which a trainee takes a rest interval of 30–90 seconds, followed by additional sets of the same movement.

Sleeve The hollow metal tube fitted over the bar of an adjustable barbell or dumbbell. This sleeve helps the bar rotate more easily in the hands during an exercise. To aid a trainee in gripping the bar when her hands are sweaty, this sleeve is usually scored with shallow crosshatched grooves called *knurlings.*

Stress The sum of all pressures placed on the human mind and body. Excessive stress can harm your health if allowed to continue for long periods of time. For optimum health, you must minimize the stresses that have become a part of your everyday life.

Weight Training A form of physical exercise using weight resistance provided by barbells, dumbbells, or exercise machines.

Weight training can be pursued toward numerous goals—bodybuilding, improving sports performance, increasing strength, competing as a weight lifter, gaining weight, slimming, rehabilitating an injury, increasing aerobic conditioning, improving health, providing a greater sense of personal well-being, etc.

Workout The program or routine of exercises (including aerobic exercise, strength training movements, and flexibility exercises) done to its completion each training day. This is also called a *training session*.

Recommended Reading

Books

Aerobics

Dreyfack, Raymond. *The Complete Book of Walking.* New York: Arco, 1979.

Lance, Kathryn. *Running for Health and Beauty: A Complete Guide for Women.* New York: The Bobbs-Merrill Company, Inc., 1977.

Lieb, Thom. *Everybody's Book of Bicycle Riding.* Emmaus, PA: Rodale Press, 1981.

Ullyot, Dr. Joan. *Women's Running.* Mountain View, CA: Anderson-World Publications, 1976.

Weiner, Harvey S. *Total Swimming.* New York: Simon and Schuster, 1980.

Anatomy

Gray, Henry. *Anatomy, Descriptive and Surgical.* London: Crown Publishers, 1968.

Flexibility

Anderson, Bob. *Stretching.* Bolinas, CA: Shelter Publications, 1980.

Uram, Paul. *The Complete Stretching Book.* Mountain View, CA: Anderson-World Publications, 1980.

Nonapparatus Exercise

Fonda, Jane. *Jane Fonda's Workout Book.* New York: Simon and Schuster, 1981.

Nutrition

Darden, Ellington, Ph.D. *The Nautilus Nutrition Book.* Chicago: Contemporary Books, 1981.

Nutrition Almanac. New York: McGraw-Hill Book Co., 1975.

Physiology

Astrand, Per-Olof, and Rodahl, Kaare. *Textbook of Work Physiology.* New York: McGraw-Hill Book Co., 1977.

Sprague, Ken. *The Athlete's Body.* Los Angeles: J. P. Tarcher, Inc., 1981.

Pregnancy and Baby Exercises

Prudden, Suzy, and Sussman, Jeffrey. *Suzy Prudden's Pregnancy & Back-to-Shape Exercise Program.* New York: Workman Publishing, 1980.

Sports Medicine

Darden, Ellington, Ph.D. *The Athlete's Guide to Sports Medicine.* Chicago: Contemporary Books, 1981.

Mirkin, Gabe, MD, and Hoffman, Marshall. *The Sportsmedicine Book.* Boston: Little, Brown and Company, 1978.

Weight Training

Barrilleaux, Doris, and Murray, Jim. *Inside Weight Training for Women.* Chicago, Contemporary Books, 1978.

Columbu, Dr. Franco, and Columbu, Dr. Anita, with Knudson, R. R. *Starbodies— The Women's Weight Training Book.* New York: E. P. Dutton, 1978.

Columbu, Franco; with Fels, George. *Winning Bodybuilding.* Chicago: Contemporary Books, 1977.

Darden, Ellington, Ph.D. *The Nautilus Book.* Chicago: Contemporary Books, 1980.

Dobbins, Bill, and Sprague, Ken. *The Gold's Gym Weight Training Book.* Los Angeles: J. P. Tarcher, Inc., 1978.

Kennedy, Robert. *Natural Body Building for Everyone.* New York: Sterling Publishing Company, Inc., 1980.

Lance, Kathryn. *Getting Strong.* Indianapolis/New York: The Bobbs-Merrill Company, Inc., 1978.

Leen, Edie. *Complete Women's Weight Training Guide.* Mountain View, CA: Anderson-World, Inc., 1980.

Mentzer, Mike, with Friedberg, Andy. *The Mentzer Method to Fitness.* New York: William Morrow and Company, Inc., 1980.

Murray, Jim. *Inside Bodybuilding.* Chicago: Contemporary Books, 1978.

Murray, Jim. *Inside Weight Lifting and Weight Training.* Chicago: Contemporary Books, 1977.

Nyad, Diana, and Hogan, Candace Lyle. *Basic Training for Women.* New York: Harmony Books, 1981.

Reynolds, Bill. *Complete Weight Training Book.* Mountain View, CA: Anderson-World, Inc., 1976.

Schwarzenegger, Arnold, with Hall, Douglas Kent. *Arnold's Bodyshaping for Women.* New York: Simon and Schuster, 1979.

Sing, Vanessa. *Lift for Life!* New York: Bolder Books, 1977.

Sprague, Ken. *The Gold's Gym Book of Strength Training for Athletes.* Los Angeles: J. P. Tarcher, Inc., 1979.

Weider, Betty, and Weider, Joe. *The Weider Book of Bodybuilding for Women.* Chicago: Contemporary Books, 1981.

Zane, Frank and Christine. *Super Bodies in 12 Weeks.* New York: Simon and Schuster, 1982.

Zane, Frank and Christine. *The Zane Way to a Beautiful Body.* New York: Simon and Schuster, 1979.

Magazines

American Health: Fitness of Body and Mind is an excellent new magazine that covers the territory outlined by its subtitle. It is published bimonthly and can be ordered from American Health Partners, 80 Fifth Avenue, Suite 302, New York City, NY, 10011. A year's subscription is $12; two year's, $22; and three, $33.

Muscle & Fitness and *Shape* are the world's leading physical fitness and self-improvement magazines. A year's subscription to *Muscle & Fitness* is $29.95; a year's subscription to *Shape* is $20. Both magazines can be ordered from Weider Health and Fitness, Inc., 21100 Erwin St., Woodland Hills, CA 91367. Both magazines are also available on most newsstands.

Outside magazine provides interesting columns and articles on outdoor activities and the equipment used to participate in them. It carries little on self-improvement or nutrition, but may be a resource for learning about the active, adventurous life of a multitude of outdoor sports. It is published seven or eight times a year by Mariah Publications Corp, 3401 West Division Street, Chicago, IL, 60651: one year, $12; two years, $22; and three years, $30. Newsstand price: $1.95.

Savvy magazine is geared toward executive women and covers such aspects as stress (at home or office), health, motherhood, and facts of life. Address subscription inquiries to SAVVY Magazine, P.O. Box 2495, Boulder, CO, 80322: one year, $12; two years, $24, and the newsstand price is only $2.

Self magazine covers health, fashion and beauty, love and sex, health and fitness, food and diet, and money and work. It is a monthly that can be ordered from *Self,* Box 5216, Boulder, CO, 80302: one year, $12; two years, $22; three years, $32; and newsstand, $1.75.

Women's Sports: For The Active American Women is a monthly publication that covers organized women's sports as well as nutrition, psychology, sports medicine, and strength training. It is the membership publication of the Women's Sports Foundation and subscriptions should be addressed to *Women's Sports,* P.O. Box 612, Holmes, PA, 19043. One year's membership/subscription is $12 and newsstand price is $1.50.

Index